NUMBER ONE

TIME AS DIMENSION AND HISTORY

HUBERT GRIGGS ALEXANDER

Copyright © 2013 Read Books Ltd.
This book is copyright and may not be
reproduced or copied in any way without
the express permission of the publisher in writing

British Library Cataloguing-in-Publication Data
A catalogue record for this book is available from the
British Library

A History of Clocks and Watches

Horology (from the Latin, Horologium) is the science of measuring time. Clocks, watches, clockwork, sundials, clepsydras, timers, time recorders, marine chronometers and atomic clocks are all examples of instruments used to measure time. In current usage, horology refers mainly to the study of mechanical time-keeping devices, whilst chronometry more broadly included electronic devices that have largely supplanted mechanical clocks for accuracy and precision in time-keeping. Horology itself has an incredibly long history and there are many museums and several specialised libraries devoted to the subject. Perhaps the most famous is the *Royal Greenwich Observatory*, also the source of the Prime Meridian (longitude 0° 0' 0"), and the home of the first marine timekeepers accurate enough to determine longitude.

The word 'clock' is derived from the Celtic words *clagan* and *clocca* meaning 'bell'. A silent instrument missing such a mechanism has traditionally been known as a timepiece, although today the words have become interchangeable. The clock is one of the oldest human interventions, meeting the need to consistently measure intervals of time shorter than the natural units: the day, the lunar month and the year. The current sexagesimal system of time measurement dates to approximately 2000 BC in Sumer. The Ancient Egyptians divided the day into two twelve-hour periods and used large obelisks to track the movement of the sun. They also developed water clocks, which had also been employed frequently by the Ancient Greeks, who called them 'clepsydrae'. The Shang Dynasty is also believed to have used the outflow water clock around the same time.

The first mechanical clocks, employing the verge escapement mechanism (the mechanism that controls the rate of a clock by advancing the gear train at regular intervals or 'ticks') with a foliot or balance wheel timekeeper (a weighted wheel that rotates back and forth, being returned toward its centre position by a spiral), were invented in Europe at around the start of the fourteenth century. They became the standard timekeeping device until the pendulum clock was invented in 1656. This remained the most accurate timekeeper until the 1930s, when quartz oscillators (where the mechanical **resonance** of a vibrating crystal is used to create an electrical signal with a very precise **frequency**) were invented, followed by atomic clocks after World War Two. Although initially limited to laboratories, the development of microelectronics in the 1960s made **quartz clocks** both compact and cheap to produce, and by the 1980s they became the world's dominant timekeeping technology in both clocks and **wristwatches**.

The concept of the wristwatch goes back to the production of the very earliest watches in the sixteenth century. Elizabeth I of England received a wristwatch from Robert Dudley in 1571, described as an arm watch. From the beginning, they were almost exclusively worn by women, while men used pocket-watches up until the early twentieth century. This was not just a matter of fashion or prejudice; watches of the time were notoriously prone to fouling from exposure to the elements, and could only reliably be kept safe from harm if carried securely in the pocket. Wristwatches were first worn by military men towards the end of the nineteenth century, when the importance of synchronizing manoeuvres during war without potentially revealing the plan to the enemy through signalling was increasingly recognized. It was clear that using pocket watches while in the heat of battle or while mounted on a horse was impractical, so officers began to strap the watches to their wrist.

The company H. Williamson Ltd., based in Coventry, England, was one of the first to capitalize on this opportunity. During the company's 1916 AGM it was noted that '...the public is buying the practical things of life. Nobody can truthfully contend that the watch is a luxury. It is said that one soldier in every four wears a wristlet watch, and the other three mean to get one as soon as they can.' By the end of the War, almost all enlisted men wore a wristwatch, and after they were demobilized, the fashion soon caught on - the British *Horological Journal* wrote in 1917 that '...the wristlet watch was little used by the sterner sex before the war, but now is seen on the wrist of nearly every man in uniform and of many men in civilian attire.' Within a decade, sales of wristwatches had outstripped those of pocket watches.

Now that clocks and watches had become 'common objects' there was a massively increased demand on clockmakers for maintenance and repair. Julien Le Roy, a clockmaker of Versailles, invented a face that could be opened to view the inside clockwork – a development which many subsequent artisans copied. He also invented special repeating mechanisms to improve the precision of clocks and supervised over 3,500 watches. The more complicated the device however, the more often it needed repairing. Today, since almost all clocks are now factory-made, most modern clockmakers *only* repair clocks. They are frequently employed by jewellers, antique shops or places devoted strictly to repairing clocks and watches.

The clockmakers of the present must be able to read blueprints and instructions for numerous types of clocks and time pieces that vary from antique clocks to modern time pieces in order to fix and make clocks or watches. The trade requires fine motor coordination as clockmakers must frequently work on devices with small gears and fine machinery, as well as an appreciation for the original art form. As is evident from this very short history of clocks and watches, over the centuries the items themselves have changed – almost out of recognition, but the importance of time-keeping has not. It is an area which provides a constant source of fascination and scientific discovery, still very much evolving today. We hope the reader enjoys this book.

CONTENTS

	Page
Introduction	5

Chapter I
Key Concepts in the Temopral Complex . . 8

Chapter II
Beginnings of Temporal Notions in Human
    Experience 22
    Calendric Time-Patterns 26
    Linguistic Evidence for Time Concepts . . 30
    Religious and Mythological Contributions
        to the Time-Concept 37

Chapter III
Temporal Dualism in Greek Philosophy . . . 45
    Plato 50
    Aristotle 55
    Post-Aristotelian Suggestions 64

Chapter IV
Christian Drama and the Renaissance of Quantity 66
    The Renaissance of Quantity and the
        Measurement of Time 71
    The Search for Objectivity 77

Chapter V
History and Science in Modern Thought . . 82
    Measure and Relativity 92

Chapter VI
Backgrounds of the Dual Perspective . . . 103
    The Place of Value 104
    Evaluating and Measuring 107
    Subjectivism and Objectivism 110
    Key Images of Time and Space . . . 113
    Key Images and Reality 116
    The Nature of Time 123

PREFATORY NOTE

The following study of the nature of temporal cognition was first commenced as a dissertation for the degree of Doctor of Philosophy at Yale University in the year 1933. Since that time, many alterations have been made, some sections being added, others deleted. In particular the initial chapter on temporal abstractions is entirely new, and incorporates a philosophy of abstraction which I have developed only in the last few years.

There is no need for a new treatise on the history of the time-concept in Occidental philosophy, after the very adequate work of J. A. Gunn, *The Problem of Time*, and the short supplemental treatise by Louise Heath, *The Concept of Time*. The present treatise is, however, more than simply a history of this concept; it is an attempt to clarify certain major philosophical questions by developing a philosophy of abstraction in connection with the concept of time, in which case we are led very curiously to a theory of the dual cognition of time. Certain connections and ramifications of this theory are developed in the last chapter.

The present work, originally presented as "The Intelligibility of Time," was commenced at the suggestion of my father, Professor H. B. Alexander, and carried on under Professor W. M. Urban, of Yale University. To these men and to Professors W. H. Sheldon and F. S. C. Northrop, of Yale, I owe the principal debt for the ideas which have gone into this work.

Grateful acknowledgments are made to Professor C. V. Newsom, of Oberlin College, and to Professor Leslie Spier, of the University of New Mexico for comments on certain portions of the treatise, also to Dean J. C. Knode, of the University of New Mexico, and to Professors Sheldon and Urban for reading the entire work in its revised form and for offering valuable criticisms.

The author wishes to make grateful acknowledgment also to the the following publishers for permissions to quote from various works: George Allen and Unwin Ltd., of London; J. M. Dent and Sons, of London and Toronto; The University of California Press, Berkeley, California; Charles Scribner's Sons, of New York; Harcourt, Brace and Company, of New York; Harper and Brothers, of New York and London; The Macmillan Company of New York; E. P. Dutton and Company of New York; Random House, Inc., of New York; The Open Court Publishing Company of Chicago, Illinois; and The Science Press, of Lancaster, Pennsylvania.

H. G. ALEXANDER.

INTRODUCTION

> What is Time? If no one asks me, I know; but if I wish to explain to one who asks, I do not know.
> (St. Augustine, *Confessions*, xi, 17)

Basic as is the factor of time in all experience, the bare concept of time is extraordinarily difficult to isolate either with clarity or conviction. Yet the question of temporal patterns is a key problem for all branches of modern science. The study of causes and types of change, whether in physical, biological, or social science, is indeed the central focus of these disciplines. The Greek conception of Nature or *Physis*, which has set the stage for subsequent scientific investigation, is well defined in Aristotle's terms as "the principle and cause of motion and rest."[1] And it is the study and cataloging of types of change or "motion," and the relating of these to some constant or "rest," which has constituted a major part of our science. But the existence of change implies some sort of temporal reality, and the measure of change requires a temporal reality which is capable of being conceived as a dimension of events, i.e., a *measurable* continuum.

Not only is it in science, however, that questions of the nature of time emerge. In the study of value, in ethics, aesthetics, and religion, another type of temporal issue arises. Man has almost instinctively associated greater value with the more enduring or immutable characteristics of his universe. The hunger for eternity, it would seem, is closely related to the hunger for values. Even Kant, we remember, considered a temporal infinity necessary for the realization of moral values.

Though the need for a clear interpretation of time is thus focal for science, religion, and philosophy, it is surprising to discover what confusions have dogged the course

---

[1] *Physics*, 192b. Translation by Wicksteed and Cornford in the Loeb Classical Library edition.

of the time-concept in European thought. Sometimes time appears only as an accompaniment of movement or change, in which case it tends to be superseded as a basic concept by that of the most regular kind of change. Sometimes it appears as the condition of change, in which all change takes place, whence it tends to disappear as itself any perceptible reality and to remain at best as only a sort of presupposed form of all perceptions. If it is presupposed as the condition of the measurement of events, time itself would not seem to be measurable, but only something intuited or felt. If, on the other hand, time is identified with some particular movement or some sense of change within the self, it can have no assured regularity, and it loses its objectivity. Time has been claimed variously to be objectively real, subjectively real, unreal; the condition of movement, dependent on movement, a type of movement, a measure of movement; a continuum, a set of atomic instants, a dimension or variable of space-time, and so forth. It is small wonder, then, that a consistent interpretation of time seems first to require the construction of a metaphysics. Indeed, a philosophical analysis of the problem must force one to certain metaphysical assumptions.

From the above set of opinions regarding time, three major problems emerge: first, what is the reality or existential status of time; second, what is its relation to movement or change; and third, what is the particular character or nature of time (i.e., is it finite or eternal, continuous or discrete, etc.). These problems lead us inevitably back to more basic epistemological and metaphysical considerations. Indeed, with regard to the epistemological question, we are confronted almost at once by two primary modes of temporal knowledge. These have already been indicated, the first being the mensurational mode, and the second the evaluational. It may very well be that this dualism represents some profound distinction with respect to knowledge itself which will lead us beyond the problem of time. It is in the consideration of the relation of time to movement or change that this dualism becomes most apparent; for here a repetitive and cyclical type of movement gives a very different perspective to our notion of time from that given by an unique and progressive type of change. It is the former orientation which enables us to measure time and to constitute of it a dimension, as in the modern notion of space-time; but it is the latter orientation which gives to time its teleological and evaluational character.

Before we study, in some of its historical manifestations, this dualism of temporal conception, we shall find it most profitable to analyze the various abstractable key images of the temporal complex. Each key image is a simplified time-trait, which when combined with the other key images in what may be termed the "temporal complex" contributes to the total notion or concept of time. When we have analyzed these bare traits we can resynthesize them with a more adequate understanding of temporal nature, and by varying each element in our resynthesis we can arrive at all the various major conceptions of time. We turn now to the undertaking of this task.

Chapter I

KEY CONCEPTS IN THE TEMPORAL COMPLEX

Our first awareness of time is an indirect one. We notice different changes, different movements, different events. These crudely give the impression of subsequent or concomitant relationships, and so gradually we construct the idea of a temporal continuum within which all changes are related. Perhaps even prior to such a construction, however, there is the impression of different types of change-pattern. On linguistic grounds, as we shall see, there is good evidence for believing in the priority of such notions in the development of most languages. It appears from this evidence that the basic mental processes of comparing and distinguishing operate as much for events as for objects, so that events also may be grouped by their similarities. These similarities are roughly what we mean by the patterns of change.

Let us posit as our most elementary concept, then, a world of concrete objects or events which may somehow be recognized as separate individuals. We may immediately add to this the notion of these individuals as parts of larger complexes, or as capable of being subdivided into smaller entities. We thus create a *part-whole* relationship which is characterized by the removable or addible nature of the part. In this sense, we imagine a page as a part of a book, and a book as a part of a library. The relationship of *quality* to *object* is different from the part-whole relation; for a quality is only capable of being imaginatively abstracted or "drawn away" from an object, whereas a part is either imaginatively or physically removable from the concrete. The quality is the product only of mental analysis, not of physical analysis. For example, the color of an object or the pattern of an event may be imagined *in abstracto*, but they are not subject to physical removal.

We now have two basic relationships: part-whole, and quality-object. We must note further that the term "quality" ordinarily refers to the more static, non-changing (though changeable) aspects of the concrete object or event. Activities and functionings, however, are also abstractable, although such abstractions become clearly conceived only after they have been reduced to the pattern of the activity (e.g., the graph of a change), which is itself static.

But not only may the part be abstracted from the whole or the quality from the object or the function from the event, but the *relation* itself may be abstracted. This applies to relations internal to the original unit (e.g., the ratio of sides to the ends of a book cover), or external (e.g., the relation of the book to the table upon which it lies). The relational abstraction, which is like the qualitative in being changeable but not changing, may be distinguished from the latter by its dependence upon two or more relata. Of course, the quality may involve internal relations (e.g., shape), but as quality it is to be viewed as a *single* aspect of the entire individual, not as a set of internal relations. We need not here decide whether qualities would better be described wholly as relations, or wholly as functions, or whether functions are reducible to relations or vice versa. It is enough that each type of abstraction—part, quality, function, or relation—gives a particular and basic point of view or perspective to the nature of the abstraction with which we are dealing.

Before we can consider the basic abstractions of the temporal complex it will be necessary to delve somewhat into the nature of abstractions. Abstractions are the result of the mental process of abstracting which is that of removing certain features for mental consideration, or perhaps better, of centering the attention upon these features to the exclusion of the rest. As stated earlier, it is the process of mental analysis.

We sometimes speak of "levels of abstraction," assuming

thereby that some abstractions are closer to the immediate empirical level, while others are further removed from it. This impression of distance from the empirical level may be reached in two ways. The first is really spurious so far as abstracting is concerned, for it depends rather upon the degree of generality of the abstraction. Now an abstraction need be abstracted from only one individual or event, but the common abstractions are those which are made from many cases, so that they also appear to be generalizations or concepts which cover a class or set of *similar* individuals. The similarity can be abstracted from all those cases, but the generalization is not itself the abstraction, it is merely dependent upon it for the logic of its grouping. That is, an abstraction is concerned with the feature abstracted, no matter from how many cases. A generalization, on the contrary, is definitely a grouping or classifying concept or term. Abstractions are graded, however, by their degree of generality. Color in general, for example, is considered a higher abstraction than blue, since all visually perceived objects have color, but only a few are blue. The terms "object" and "event" are themselves generalizations of a high order; for "object" commonly refers to all ordinarily separable or individually conceivable entities in the universe, and "event" denotes all individually conceivable bits of change. It is well known that as a generalization becomes more universal or inclusive the number of common abstractable traits between the individuals becomes fewer. This may account for the impression that these traits, when abstracted, seem far removed from the concrete situation.

There is another way, however, in which abstractions may be graded. Commencing again with the concrete situation in all its complexity, the process of analysis consists in separating out the various abstractable traits. Many times, however, what is at first taken to be a single abstractable trait, upon further analysis, is itself divided up, so that we get abstractions from abstractions. For example, we might abstract the rectangular shape from a book cover, and then abstract right-angleness from the total rectangle. This process, if carried on far enough, would leave us with certain *minimal traits* or *end-concepts*, which form the limits of the abstractive process in the sense that beyond them or from them no meaningful abstraction can be made. They are the simplest abstractions, but at the same time they are the furthest from the concrete situation.

There are two basic mental processes which must be added to those of abstracting and generalizing. The first of these is that of *negating* abstractions. The act of negating or denying an abstraction has the effect of throwing our attention over to the residue or left-over set of traits as they would exist without the particular abstracted trait. This process, as we shall see, is invaluable. The second process is that of *manipulating* abstractions, especially by extending or reducing continua, or by adding or subtracting discreta. For example, the concept of infinity may be derived either by abstracting the trait of limit, and then negating this abstraction (which is the etymological meaning of the word), or it may be derived by extending the abstracted trait of continuity. Eternity, likewise, may be the result of the negation of temporal limits, or the extension of the temporal continuum. An infinitesimal point or a "knife-edge" present may be the result of a simple negation of magnitude or duration, or it may result from the reduction of these concepts until the end-point or limit of this process is reached. It should be noted that the negation of the concept of space itself would leave no place in which to locate even a spaceless point, and the negation of time would leave no temporal now at all, but complete timelessness; for the terms "space" and "time" are used to cover the entire complex of spatial and temporal traits.

The notions of infinity and eternity further serve to illustrate the presence of the end-concept. Thus, we speak of a series or an extension as approaching infinity as its limit, when the meaning of an infinite series is to have no limit. In this there is a tacit recognition that the concept of infinity (or eternity) is only meaningful as the suggested limit of a process of removing or surpassing limits. We know how difficult it is to give to infinity or eternity a positive or readily imagined referent. Is it not because these are end-concepts of processes of abstractive manipulation? An infinite continuum has the minimal trait of lacking limits, and the process of extending magnitudes beyond all imaginable limits reaches the end of this type of imagining when it has simply negated all ultimate limits. Here we have the thought-limit of a process which denies limits!

Considering time specifically, we notice first that it does not bear a part-whole relation with other elements in our experience. That is, it cannot be physically removed as a concrete individual and studied as a single object in experience. It is to such an extent a concomitant of all experience that we are immediately inclined to regard it as an abstraction from all experience. However, we are more aware of time passage in cases of activity and change, so that we tend to think of time as an abstraction from change. But change is itself an abstraction from experience; for experience includes the relatively permanent and the relatively changing which even the early Greeks abstract from each other as two qualities of reality. Why, we may well ask, should time be thought of more in connection with change than with permanence? It would seem to be that complete Parmenidean permanence verges upon timelessness, indicating that awareness of time is somehow interwoven with awareness of change. If change is an abstraction from events and time an abstraction from change, then time is an abstraction of an abstraction, which places it both for this reason and for its universality on a high abstractive level.

Let us revert to the common sense level, and review the process in somewhat more detail. Our earliest awareness is not of change as such, or time alone, but of particular changes and events. We use the term "time" ordinarily to refer to (1) the interval between events, (2) the duration of an event, (3) the moment of occurrence, (4) the rate of speed or "tempo" of an event, or (5), by transference, the events themselves (e.g., "hard times," "good time," etc.). In the case of recurring events, we speak of "times" as the moments of repeated occurrence. If this recurrence is in any way regular or habitual, we may speak of "the time" for it to occur.

Further analysis indicates several basic contrasts. First, there is the opposition between *momentary* and *durative*. Primitively this contrast seems to be simply that of relatively short events as against relatively long ones. If we supply the notion of a durational continuum, however, we can further distinguish the moment or instant from the continuum, as in the spatial analogue the intersecting mark is distinguished from the continuous line.

A second contrast may be noted as between the duration of an *event* and the duration of the *interval* between events. Psychologically this distinction seems due to a feeling of a period of relative activity as against a period of rest or inactivity. During a period of activity the attention is on the event itself with its transitional or changing factors emphasized. During a period of rest, however, the attention is on the uninterrupted flow of durational passage with a tinge of anticipation for the beginning of the next period of activity and the end of the interval. Routine and habitual activities, be it noted, tend to be reduced to the impression of continual flow (interval), whereas tense, exciting, and dramatic activities give a stronger impression of transition (event). The notion of static permanence or persistence, then, is closely linked to the idea of temporal interval, the period between active events. The impression of change, transition, novelty, on the other hand, is linked with the event itself.

Another contrast exists between the *sameness* of repeated events and the *novelty* of different events. Repeated events in human experience are routine events, and as has been said they tend to appear as continual flow or interval. Indeed, we shall see that the connection between repetition and interval in temporal character is very close on the abstract side as well. Novelty, on the contrary, is connected with transition, for it is the differentiation of an end condition from an initial condition which marks transitional character. And novelty, we note, must be due to the impression of successive difference. Even in repetition, of course, there must theoretically be some small degree of novelty, otherwise there would be no way of distingushing successive events at all and hence there would be no separate units to be similar to each other, but we should have simple permanence again. However, the impression of repetition is due to an ignoring of novelty and a focusing of the attention upon the recurrent similarities, whereas transitional awareness demands a clear feeling of difference rather than of sameness.

So far our investigation has led to a number of contrasting qualities which are ordinarily associated with the concept of time. These qualities may be refined until we consider only their minimal traits, that is, until they become end-concepts. Such a procedure will enable us to understand better the precise focus or perspective which each concept gives to the time-complex. But it must be remembered that end-concepts in themselves are only key images, governing points of view, which need the other qualities of any complex to give them a useful meaning.

Duration alone—we may call it "pure duration" if we remember that we are in no way yet concerned with the Bergsonian problem of subjectivity and objectivity—is with difficulty refined into an end-concept; for it is very dependent upon other members of this complex. It might be described negatively as that which keeps the limits of a temporal interval apart or admits of the separating of the initial and final stage of a transition. In more positive terms, it is simply the bare awareness of the persistence of experience. It can neither be completely changeless (mere *permanence*) nor completely changing (mere *transition*); for these are two other end-concepts in the temporal complex. But duration is required both by permanence and transition. The real contrast with duration would be *momentaneousness*, which by itself would deny both transition and permanence. The pure end-concepts of duration, momentaneousness, transition, and permanence are all absurd as sole qualifications of experience. Nevertheless, they do appear as possible distinguishable qualities, and as such are useful in an intellectual analysis of temporal experience.

To note in somewhat more detail the interdependence of these concepts, moment, as a completely durationless instant, either demands a durational continuum in which to be placed, or else negates duration altogether, in which case it ceases to have position and becomes almost completely meaningless. Duration, on the other hand, even as a mere continuum, needs a recognition of some kind of continuity, which in this case means a perception of before-and-afterness. But before-and-afterness implies transition or successive differences, which in turn demands recognition of moments of different states, and so we arrive back at moments by way of transition. Extreme permanence, or perfect staticity, loses any basis for continuation which requires, as we have said, an awareness of succession or change. Extreme transition is likewise absurd when pushed to the limit of absolute novelty; for there also all continuity is lost in a series of fragmented episodes which are not properly even a series.

The concept of *interval* is merely that of limits or units which serve to mark off any kind of continuum. Temporal character is given to an interval by the durational quality of the continuum. If this continuum is conceived as completely homogeneous there is nothing intrinsic to determine an interval or unit. Like inches or centimeters, the temporal interval is placed arbitrarily upon the continuum for quantitative or measuring purposes.

Repetition involves a recognizable unit which may be taken in a serial aspect, and hence it is dependent upon some interval. An interval-unit is repeatedly applied to a continuum to give it the measured character of a *dimension*. The clock is our obvious model of the repetition of a durational interval-unit. Any device, however, which we believe to indicate a sequence of regular intervals, the sameness being that of equivalent lengths only, would suffice to give us a measure of duration.

Temporal repetition, however, is not necessarily of the foregoing type. It may mean a recurrence of definite event patterns, where something in the internal nature of the event itself is responsible for the similarity. Thus, historical cycles, life cycles, etc., are dependent not upon the mere length of time which is consumed, but upon the event character. In such cases the limits of the transition (e.g., birth and death) are the marks of an interval as well. But from the point of view of a transition of a certain kind; it is the recurrent pattern of birth-life-death that gives a similarity, and not the number of years consumed by the process. The progress of cultures may be marked off into characteristic, epochs which have enough similarity to warrant the application of the notion of repetition. But in all such cases of repetition, it is not the external limits imposed by a selected duration-measurer or interval-unit, but the internal nature of the events themselves, which give rise to the idea of repeated cycles.

Tempo depends on the relating of two or more repeated units (whether of the interval or of the transitional kind) in order to determine the relative frequency of recurrence. The concept of tempo is used in music to indicate the number of ticks or beats per interval of clock time. However, there may be a type of internal or transitional tempo due to the feeling of tension or suspense within the event itself quite irrespective of the relative measure of duration.[1]

Duration is often characterized as a *unidirectional* continuum in which the movement is *irreversible*. But unidirectionality and irreversibility would seem to depend primarily upon the before-after character which is distinguishable only in transition. The frame of reference which enables us to think of directionality in a temporal dimension is surely the awareness of successive *novel* differences. Mere successive difference might be an alternation, as of a pendulum, from one position to another and back again. But every event in experience is colored with some novel association, and this is true even of successive positions of a pendulum, so that the quality of novelty appears to be the principal basis of the unidirectional time-aspect.

The notion of *past-present-future* is sometimes regarded as the basic concept of the temporal complex. It can be related, however, to the irreversible durational continuum with some particular point or event considered as the present, thus affording a frame of reference for dividing past from future. This concept of course looms much larger in the problem of temporal reality, in which connection it can be considered more profitably.

It remains only to expand what has already been indicated with respect to the notion of *eternity*. If we remove all character from duration except complete changeless permanence, we might conceive it as limitless, but it would have to be also eventless. This verges, of course, upon the absurdity of a Parmenidean static universe. However, if we grant some degree of transition or change, we immediately require an end-limit toward which the change approaches. We may negate this limit, so that it is indefinitely postponed and never quite reached. If we remove it altogether we lose the quality of transition, which, as we have seen, requires a beginning and an end, and we return

---

[1]. See Chapter II, especially pp. 23-24, 36, and 39.

to pure static duration. Hence, we find a paradox within the notion of eternity.

Another idea of eternity, the timeless eternity of Greek philosophy, may be reached by negating directly the dynamic or transitional character of events, so that we have left only the pattern or "form" of change, which in effect eliminates duration altogether. When Plato defines time as a "moving image of eternity," it seems that he is trying to make dynamic again this static patterned eternity.[2] That is, he is trying to reintroduce the durative-transitional trait.

There is a strong temptation, almost an intellectual necessity, to give to some one concept out of a complex, such as the temporal complex, a dominant position, that is, to regard some one trait as representing the basic reality upon which we now superimpose the other traits. Let us not fall too quickly into this mode of thought, however, for these concepts may all be equal abstractions from the total complex situation which is our genuine reality. It is saner to regard these purified end-concepts as possible key images or perspectives useful in focusing our attention upon the various aspects of experience. We may, nevertheless, try out in turn these concepts as if each were the dominant one in the complex.

The concept of duration focuses our attention upon what may seem the most abstract quality of the complex, namely, pure endurance plus a slight tinge of succession or before-and-afterness. A stronger focus upon before-and-afterness or past-present-future turns our attention to transition, and a definite idea of sequence turns our attention to interval, but if we wish we may focus our attention away from these traits back to that of a duration that is as nearly free of them as possible. Whichever concept is taken as the key image, it will give us a new perspective on the others. If interval is stressed, we arrive at the notion of time as a dimension. If transition is stressed, we find that time has

---

2. See pp. 51-52.

more the character of a set of events. Indeed, it appears that not only different meanings of "time" but different theories of temporal nature are due in large part to varying emphases within this temporal complex.

The terms "time" and "change" themselves often reflect different emphases or focuses within a complex of experienced traits which are very closely linked together. Change is concerned with types of patterned activity in which the beginning and end forms of a transition are fairly clear-cut. Time is concerned more with the durative ground of these activities. Yet pure duration or pure transition are end-concepts which need each other to give meaning to themselves.

The various patterns of change, which emerge from experience as the more universal types, necessitate the different emphases or perspectives which we give to time itself. For example, in the case of history and drama which constitute a major part of our experience we find that the internal transitional nature of the event is all-important. It is the beginning and ending, the anticipatory conditions and the climax, which give the poignancy and meaning to historical and dramatic character. Folktales which end lamely with an "and they lived happily ever after" bear witness to the incongruity for drama of endless or uneventful duration. But neither is it the measured sequence of external intervals which gives meaning to drama. Aristotle's unities notwithstanding, it is certainly not the number of years that the story covers which gives it its meaning. Thus, the tale of a few hours or the tale of several centuries may offer the same type of climax. Where dramatic event and activity is concerned, the attention is centered primarily upon the transitional time-trait, and time becomes essentially a change or transition.

On the other hand, where routine is the prime consideration, or where change means only the study and measuring of relative motions and repetitions, it is not the transitional, but the intervaled nature of time which is central. Our attention is turned to the measuring of a durational ground by some extremely regular movement (such as the rotation of the earth). Time now becomes primarily a dimension, i.e., a measurable continuum. Certain types of experience emphasize this aspect. For example, all matters of habit and routine are worked out by the season, day, or clock, and we get the impression that time is but a sequence of repetitions.

The durational ground is by itself unsatisfactory either for dramatic experience or for routine experience. In the first case, a feeling of beginning and end, of mounting tensions and a final breaking, gives emphasis to the transitional temporal trait. In the second case, a feeling of simple recurrence and repetition, of going over and over the same thing, gives emphasis to the interval and repetition of time. But in either case the durational ground is granted as the actuality which allows potentialities for transition to be realized, or as the continuum which allows the potentiality of measurement to become actual.

Even in present-day science, we find these two types of change influencing two different conceptions of time. The biological and geological sciences, with their modern evolutional interest, require a long-range concept of process akin to that of human history but much more vast. The traits of this concept are its unending succession of changes or transitions, lack of repetition, and continuous creativity or novelty. Inasmuch as the social sciences depend to a large measure upon history, they also must view change in this fashion (even though they sometimes attempt the other type with absurd results). The other sciences for the most part, following the example of physics, interpret isolated events by their temporal measurement and uniformities of pattern. In this case, repetition, far from being subordinated, is the prime center of attention. Cycles and recurrences, rather than transition and novelty, are the character-giving traits. And these diverse impressions of temporal requirements influence divergent interpretations of time itself, leaving within the body of science an implicit contradiction.[3]

The concept of time itself has evolved. Its meaning appears to have vacillated within the complex of traits outlined above. The external activities of mankind, involving experience with particular changes and particular routines, have thrown this concept into one or another form and given it a somewhat different character for different enterprises. Let us, then, examine some of these characteristic enterprises and some of the corresponding forms of the time concept; for in that way we shall see more clearly how time is related to change, and change to experience.

---

3. See H. Miller, *History and Science* (Berkeley, Calif., Univ. of Calif. Press. 1939.)

Chapter II

BEGINNINGS OF TEMPORAL NOTIONS IN HUMAN EXPERIENCE

Temporal patterns in human experience are extraordinarily varied. Each activity gives rise to its own form of change, which in turn influences the temporal concept based upon that activity. We cannot study each act of man, but we can divide human activities and enterprises into large groupings for the sake of convenience.

In general, we may assume that the patterns of human behavior which are either widespread or basic preoccupations of human society are those which have the greater influence upon the formation of key concepts. Primitive preoccupations with bodily and economic needs have left their impress strongly upon primitive thinking. The methods of satisfying these needs, for putting oneself in the proper and propitious contact with the powers of the world, have also contributed heavily to the conceptualizing of experience.

Nevertheless, the need for economy of thought and expression is such that the key concepts, having received conventional linguistic stability, are automatically transferred to many other events. For example, the human need for carrying a shield is transferred to the sun god, and the disk of the sun may be regarded as a shield borne by the real sun, who may be an Apollo riding in a chariot. The needs of human life are quickly applied to cosmic matters, until the cosmos itself has most of the traits of human life, perhaps even a beginning and an ending.

A culture is an extremely complex network of the qualities attending group behavior. The notion of culture is difficult to define precisely because of its complexity and because of the resulting inability to grasp it adequately by any

TIME AS DIMENSION AND HISTORY   [23

organized abstracting of these qualities. However, a culture acquires a special character of its own as the result of certain governing concepts and values which tend to overshadow the others. There may be a conflict of these concepts and values such that the dominant ones simply hold the lesser in check, or there may be an integration so that the lesser become subordinated harmoniously to the greater.

We might expect a close connection between the chief source of economic support of a people and the set of dominant concepts. The economic support, especially the food supply, is naturally of paramount concern to man. However, there seems to be something more subtle or more profound than this at work organizing thought patterns into certain grooves which would not be predictable simply on the basis of a typical economy. It may be only a matter of chance that some peoples hit upon one set of key ideas while another group organizes its experience differently. In our present state of knowledge it would indeed be presumptuous to go further than this in an attempt to discover the causes at work.

Of course there are connections between economic type and conceptual type. With respect to temporal concepts, we may illustrate this by mentioning that a hunting or fishing economy will determine the concept of temporal interval and epoch largely by the habits of the game. This is borne out particularly by a study of primitive calendars. On the other hand, linguistic analysis apparently carries us back to a more primitive psychological level of conceptual orientation.

There is one way especially, however, in which hunting or fishing enterprises will influence temporal concepts. These enterprises give rise to a strong feeling of expectancy. The purposive nature of all practices leading up to the capture of the game or fish produces naturally a strong awareness of the internal character of events. The emerging concept is distinctly teleological. Concepts and rituals of a people who are primarily hunters or fishers will turn largely upon the drama of this food-enterprise, and this drama may easily become the image of the entire drama of life itself, both human and cosmic. In hunting and fishing, periods of alertness and full consciousness are habitually followed, often none too regularly, by periods of complete inertia. A sense of time passage as we noted in Chapter I, comes rather with a period of bodily alertness and consciousness than with a semi-soporific state. So we may find in this characteristic of hunters and fishers the kernel of the dramatic and transitional feeling of time.

The dominance of a dramatic concept of time for the primitive hunter is further indicated by his tendency to designate epochs by outstanding events.[1] Not only the seasonal habits of his primary foodstuff, but the development of the individual to the point of certain accomplishments, or the occurrence of certain unusual and dramatic events in the group life will give him points to which he may tie his chronology. His concept of time, half-conscious though it may be, can roughly be outlined as one which sees duration not with the invariable continuity of our own abstract idea, but with a seasonal pulsation marked by the irregular occurrence of important events in individual and tribal life.

When we consider the possible differences introduced by a group which depends primarily upon domesticated plants or animals for its subsistence, we find that the increasing control over nature requires increased development of a calendar. Observation of stars and the movements of the solar system afford the most obvious source for such calculations. Indeed, the nocturnal vigils of primarily pastoral peoples undoubtedly contributed to the development of purely astronomical calendars among such peoples. Agricultural economies, however, tend to follow seasonal changes

---

1. See, for example, Roth, "An Introductory Study of the Arts, Crafts, and Customs of the Guiana Indians," *38 Annual Report*, BAE, p. 715.

marked by a botanical orientation. The difference, for example, between the ancient Egyptian calendar which based its annual measure upon the inundation of the Nile as against the Babylonian calendar which was astronomical, may be taken as illustrative of this diverse orientation.

Once an astronomical calendar becomes established, time concepts converge rapidly upon the cyclical and measured notion with which we ourselves are primarily familiar. Indeed, as man becomes more and more independent of environmental variations through the growth of commerce and industry, he tends to regulate his life by astronomical and mechanical time measurers, interpreting all types of periods in terms of these. The culmination of this tendency appears in the concept of time as pure continuous duration subject to any type of division which one may care to impose upon it. At this stage the inner, transitional, or dramatic quality of time is but vaguely remembered in a few surviving beliefs. Our concept of Father Time, for example, with his close association with death as a terminal event of our lives may be considered as such a remnant. Aristotle is himself not quite free of the feeling that time is a destructive force, thus giving it more character than should be ascribed to an empty continuum.[2] It is well to remember in this connection that Aristotle's early interests were largely biological.

As the preponderant activity of a group or society becomes more commercial and industrial and less concerned with life patterns, so the concept of time becomes more rigidly mechanical. It is thought of in terms of external intervals arbitrarily imposed which contain equivalent amounts of time-passage or duration. The dramatic and transitional sense of time becomes less and in some cases disappears completely. Activities which are regulated by clocks, especially "time clocks," or which are determined solely with reference to measured intervals, have given rise

---

2. Cf. *Physics*, 221 b.

to time as a continuously ticked-off duration within which events of varying lengths may take place. This concept is indeed far from the primitive association of time with the pregnant, expectant, transitional, and dramatic character which the life-image produces. In hunting, pastoral, and even in agricultural enterprises, the life period is so paramount that *it* determines the epoch of life-cycle, and not the reverse.

CALENDRIC TIME-PATTERNS

We have already indicated that astronomical calendars are not the most primitive. They are late-comers in the process of time-measurement. Peoples who depend for their subsistence primarily upon game or growing plants measure their time principally in terms of these. The simple primitive interests of man are matters of food, shelter, and clothing; and the seasonal changes which affect these are the first indications of time to be counted. The days of the year are too numerous to be useful as a unit of time to men who can scarcely count at all. The earliest calendars more often take lunar periods as a basis for calculating time. The month may start with any phase of the moon, and last until the next similar phase. But more significant than the elemental nature of the lunar period is the fact that the successive lunations were named according to natural phenomena which occurred during them.

The calendars of the American Indians north of Mexico, for example, are often of what Leona Cope calls the "descriptive" type.[3] By this she means that the lunar periods are named or "described" by some important event in the migratory or life cycle. Terms such as "Russetback thrush month" or "Flying ant month," or "Big leaf month" are typical. In a study of the arts, crafts, and customs of the Guiana Indians, W. E. Roth makes an observation of a trait which is characteristic of primitive descriptive calen-

---

3. Leona Cope, "Calendars of the Indians North of Mexico," *University of California Publications in American Archaeology and Ethnology*, Vol. 16, No. 4.

dars. He says, "The year is divided not into months but into seasons according as the more important economic animals and plants after which they are named breed, reach maturity, bear fruit, etc. These seasons follow each other in regular succession year by year, according as certain stars and constellations make their appearance, take up a certain position in the sky, or even disappear. That is to say, the presence and position of various stars are associated with particular seasons. More than this, each such star is the permanent home of, in fact actually is, the spirit of that same flesh, fowl, tree, or plant which is then in season, and into which it changes or passes."[4] Whether biological events are associated with lunar phases or with stellar positions, as in this latter example, the connection between periods of time and migrations or maturations is distinctive. We can readily comprehend the early ties made between astronomical and terrestrial phenomena. Astrology, for example, is a remnant of this association.

Temporal periods are not always associated with biological or astronomical events in primitive societies. In some cases social or ritual events predominate. These, of course, may in turn be based on natural phenomena, but in these cases the use of the natural phenomena is secondary. The Hopi, for example, are reported to divide their calendar according to ceremonies. Or, perhaps better, this characteristic is represented by the winter counts of the Plains Indians, which it is thought were set down as an aid to the memory in reviewing tribal history.[5] The years (or months) are represented by heavy lines (drawn on buckskin or some other suitable material) with a pictograph attached to each line to indicate the event of outstanding significance to the tribe for that particular period. Thus, by referring to this chart, one would be able to say that a marriage or a death

---

4. Roth, *op. cit.* pp. 715-6. Cf. also A. I. Hallowell, "Temporal Orientation, etc.," *American Anthropologist*, No. 8, Vol. 39, No. 4, Pt. 1.

5. Cf. James Mooney, "Calendar History of the Kiowa," *17th Annual Report*, BAE, Pt. 1.

occurred so many years ago at the time of the indicated event. Personal events are thus associated with larger tribal events which can be easily remembered. This sort of tying of time by means of events is an essential feature for any calendar insofar as all calendars need points of reference (e.g., birth of Christ, founding of Rome, the Hegira, etc.)

Of even greater interest is the fact that herein we have time told off by a series of *events,* whatever the nature of those events. Time is really not divided into externally bounded periods or "chunks," as we are prone to conceive it. Rather it is marked by the internal event-quality of the period. The chief interest is not in the exact duration of a period or in the knowledge of the number of periods which have elapsed since the event, but in the association of one event with another. The primitive mind seems to be more interested, that is, in the associating of events than in the telling of time, as we conceive it.

Professor Abel Rey, in his discussion of the awakening of scientific and mathematical thought, asserts that the most primitive quantitative impression will not be truly quantitative at all, but "in place of number, even ordinal number, there will appear to be a feeling of totality which is implicit, confused, necessarily qualitative, prior to a sense of unity and multiplicity, prior to a sense of a series, and, of course, prior to a sense of a sum."[6] From this basic qualitative appreciation, which is more nearly a mere separation of the *whole* and the *less-than-whole,* has grown the sense of unity and multiplicity, of ordinal and cardinal number, although of these latter he believes the ordinal or serial came first. That is to say, the first counting was a temporally ordered process in which a sound or gesture was given as corresponding to an object or event taken one after another. The cardinal concept of a numbered aggregate, of a given quantity of objects existing simultaneously in a group, is a

---

6. *La science orientale avant les Grecs* (Paris: La Renaissance du Livre, 1930), p. 439.

later development. Of course, we must realize that this primitive ordinal numbering, illustrated for example by the counting of sheep (e.g., Polyphemus in the *Odyssey*), involves no well-developed notion of a series as such. It is merely a primitive recognition of quantity by assigning a position in a temporal sequence.

The calendar was undoubtedly one of the strongest contributors to the development of such an ordinal count. Because of the failure of the observable astronomical movements to be evenly divisible by one another, complicated calculations were required at an early stage in the development of astronomical calendars. This is well illustrated by the Egyptian calendar, for example, which developed from a lunar and solar year of twelve months with five intercalary days. To this was added the famous Sothic Cycle based on the correlation of the Sirius year (a sidereal year counted by the position of the star Sirius) with the vague solar year, giving 1460 Sirius years for 1461 solar years.[7] When cycles of this complexity were developed, a change of thought would naturally take place, so that the serial image would gradually be replaced by an image of groups of years. Temporal units would be thus more strongly likened to and thought of in terms of spatial entities, clearing the way for a further spatialization of the time concept. This further spatialization occurs when we come to take time in "chunks" or periods which for calendric purposes are exact equivalents. We must consider this process as resulting in the emphasis upon time as quantified and as a measurable something, a character which it has had strongly in ancient Greek and modern European thought.[8]

The development of the calendar has certainly had a strong influence on the concept of time. The ultimate astronomical and mechanical methods of correlating temporal phenomena have given us the impression that time is a

---

7. Cf. Norman Lockyer, *The Dawn of Astronomy* (Macmillan, 1894), pp. 24-25.
8. See on Aristotle, especially pp. 56-57.

measured continuum or dimension of the same order as spatial dimensions. Nevertheless, no calendar can successfully free itself entirely from some reference point, and at least in that reference point we have a reminder of the earlier event-quality of temporal determination. Yet, even here, the event itself comes to be considered as incidental and somewhat arbitrary, as only a convenient point from which to calculate; so that, in the end, we appear to have traveled far from the level of the primitive in the matter of calendric computations.

Linguistic Evidence for Time Concepts

In language we come directly into contact with the spirit of man as it assembles its experiences in consciousness, and attempts to give them communicable form. Language is not so much an index of the psychology of individuals as it is of group psychology, for it represents that part of man's experience which has succeeded in becoming the communicable property of many individuals. There is no doubt that language is in a sense the background and basis for the thinking of the individual, if we mean by this that language emphasizes certain facts and distinctions, so that the thought of the individual naturally falls into these channels. But it is also true that language is a medium of great flexibility, which is continually changed by the growth of thought. The invention of words, the use of metaphor and allegory, the fitting of words into different structural patterns and molds (as, for example, changing a word from one part of speech to another), each with its special connotation, are all means of transforming a language to fit one's thoughts. A language, then, will not only indicate the mental bias or perspective of a people, but it will change and develop as this perspective shifts, as new relations and information force themselves into expression.

It may be that the connection between language and other cultural forms exists only in the vaguest way,[9] but it is certain that linguistic forms of any language or dialect taken by themselves indicate the mental outlook and attitude of those people who have come to employ such language or dialect. It matters not whether the language imposes the forms of thought, or whether the forms of thought mold the language, or whether, which is more probable, the influence is interactive. Differences of dialect and difficulties of transliteration are enough evidence in themselves for the fact that languages do present mental attitudes which may be radically dissimilar. We cannot hope to canvass all the linguistic dissimilarities which are pertinent to the various modes of temporal conceptualization. Nevertheless, we can draw some broad inferences from outstanding differences.

Let us consider first the Indo-European family of languages. This family constitutes a wide and variegated group, not so compact as Semitic or Athabascan for example, but nevertheless possessing a certain pattern, a certain order and feeling of construction which is distinctive within all of its various forms. Comparatively speaking, the Indo-European languages are distinguished by a well-developed tense system. For the purpose of temporal conceptualization this is a fact of tremendous significance. Where other languages have tended to systematize the *aspect* systems,[10] Indo-European has favored a systematized *tense* system.

The primary difference between a tense system and an aspect system turns upon the emphasis given to verb forms expressing present, past, and future, as against forms which express durational, momentaneous, continuative, repetitive,

---

9. Cf. E. Sapir. *Language* (N. Y.: Harcourt Brace & Co., 1921), pp. 233 ff. Also W. Graff, *Language and Languages*, pp. 338 ff.

10. Cf. Sapir, *op. cit.*, p. 114, note 22. "A term borrowed from Slavic grammar [which has a more definite aspect system than other I.-E. languages]. It indicates the lapse of action, its nature from the standpoint of continuity. Our 'cry' is indefinite as to aspect, 'be crying' is durative, 'cry out' is momentaneous, 'burst into tears' is inceptive, 'keep crying' is continuative, 'start in crying' is durative-inceptive, 'cry now and again' is iterative, 'cry out every now and then' or 'cry in fits and starts' is momentaneous-iterative, etc."

etc., qualities of the activity or condition designated by the verb. The tense system implies the notion of a single temporal continuum divided by a moving present into past and future. The aspect system implies rather a set of temporal qualities which actions and states possess customarily, or sometimes peculiarly. In the first case, attention is turned to the relating of events to each other in a single temporal continuum. In the second case, more interest is shown in the peculiar temporal quality of the single event. The relating of events to each other is often handled in a haphazard and careless manner by languages which are primarily aspective. Aspects of time refer to the quality or state of an act as beginning, transforming, enduring, finishing, recurring, moving away from, tending towards, and so forth. Such temporal aspects may be applied anywhere in the tense scheme, either in the past, or in the future.

Closely connected with both aspect and tense systems is the modal system. This system indicates the subjective attitude which the speaker may have with regard to an event. Possibility, probability, capability, desirability, necessity, and their opposites are modal expressions. In English, for example, "I sing" is not so much the present tense of the verb "to sing" as it is a potential mode. It indicates the ability of the subject to perform the act, and with respect to tense or aspect this form is indefinite. The action may take place at any time, and it may be done once or repeatedly, for a long time or for a short time, it may have just begun or just finished. However, "I sing!" is present, but it is secondarily present, the primary emphasis being on the dramatic quality which surrounds the moment. We might call this the "dramatic mode." The true English present would be "I am singing." But this form is not only present, it is also durative in aspect, and undefined with respect to mode (i.e., "indicative," which means that it is uttered as a matter of fact without any mental reservations).

However, the most systematically developed temporal

characteristic of the English verb is now the tense system. Aspect and modal qualifications are usually turned by means of idioms and circumlocutions using prepositions, adverbs, and modal auxiliary verbs. Thus, the verb "to do" is subject to very many such qualifications, as "I do it many times," etc. Even the tense system, nevertheless, is weak in its future forms. There are many more discriminations in the past tenses (imperfect, preterit, perfect, pluperfect, etc.) than there are in the future. And there is less consistency in forming futures among Indo-European languages than in forming past tenses. For example, English and Danish use modal auxiliary verbs of wishing (will) to indicate futurity, whereas German, a close cognate, prefers the simple verb of becoming (werden). Moreover, the Romance languages abandoned the classical Latin future for a form based on the infinitive plus the verb "to have." This instability in the future indicates most likely the feeling of doubt with which any definite forecast of future events is accompanied. It therefore acquires a modal quality beyond that of the other tenses, and in a sense disrupts the absolute uniformity of the implied temporal continuum.

The basic temporal distinction in many non-Indo-European languages is simply that of completed as against not-yet-completed action (i.e., perfective and imperfective). This may be considered more a distinction of aspect than of tense. It is not so much a question of relating events to each other as it is of giving a quality to the event. In its simplest form, this distinction is that of "going on" or present as against finished or not-present.

We must be cautious in regarding the tense system as the necessary descendant of more primitive aspect and modal systems. While there may be sufficient evidence[11] of such a development within Indo-European languages, there is certainly no evidence that this is a necessary evolution. We

---

11. Cassirer, *Philosophie der Symbolischen Formen* (Berlin: Bruno Cassirer Verlag, 1923), Vol. I, pp. 166-180. Especially p. 178.

say, of course, that a tense system gives a more simplified logical impression of temporal relations, thus offering greater opportunity for a logically consistent language. But it may be that this desire for logical consistency which seems to us the natural goal of all languages is only a peculiar interest or prejudice of ours, and that other elaborations may give equally valid impressions of temporal reality.

Ernst Cassirer believes that he can distinguish three stages in the development of the linguistic time concept. The first is based on a direct spatial perception of the *present* as against the *not-present,* the here and the not-here. In support of this contention he mentions the fact that the Rwiwe-speaking people have the same adverb for yesterday and tomorrow, and the Bashambara use the same word for the distant future and the distant past. Now this is perfectly true with respect to the particular words in question; but Bantu languages have a word order which is as cranky as German, and it happens that the difference between tomorrow and yesterday, or between the future and the past is expressed by the word order. (We might compare this to the habit of French in using *"Tout à l'heure"* to refer to past or future depending upon the tense of the verb). Hence, though it may be the nature of the Negro to worry little about temporal relations, it is impossible to argue that he imagines time as a sort of spatial entity. With more justification it could be said that he does not differentiate carefully between the spatial and temporal qualifications of different acts, events, objects, etc.

The second stage which Cassirer proposes would include the distinctions of the aspect system. He mentions completed versus uncompleted action, and enduring versus passing action. The third and final stage comes with the notion of time as pure abstract concept of order. "These already presuppose some form of time measurement, and they accordingly grasp time as a sharply defined quantity-value."[12]

---
12. *Ibid.,* p. 180

However, for Cassirer, the highest developed time-consciousness is found in a reversion to an image of action whose dynamic quality resides in the moving subject and whose meaning is found in the goal toward which it is moving. This emphasis upon an inner teleological meaning must be respected, whatever we may think of Cassirer's theory of the stages of linguistic evolution.

Different languages apparently evolve in different directions. For Indo-European languages, however, there is a certain uniformity of progression which leads to a simplification of earlier confusions through an insistence upon logic as a necessary linguistic aid.[13] So far as the western Indo-European languages are concerned, the desire for logicality can be traced to the Greeks whose greatest gift was just this development of human rationality. Their penchant for logical consistency must have done much to create the impression among later European generations that all temporal concepts are best reduced to that of simple dimensionality, thus weeding out the more internal and transitional characteristics which had so long been connected with the time-quality of events.

By contrast with this dominant European time-view, there is the very interesting testimony and analysis of Hopi time concepts by the late B. L. Whorf.[14] He shows that linguistically the Hopi have no objectification or spatialization of the time-concept such as we do. They have no noun (substantive) for *time,* no tense system of past-present-future but only a designation of "earlier and later," no cardinal notion of times or days in groups, but only an ordinal notion of event series related with respect to earlier and later; in fact, they have no objectified temporal nouns at all, such as summer, winter, etc., but only adverbial ele-

---

13. Cf. Lévy-Bruhl, *Les fonctions mentales dans les sociétés inférieures* (Paris: Alcan, 1910), p. 12.
14. "The Relation of Habitual Thought and Behavior to Language," in *Language, Culture, and Personality* (Menasha, Wisconsin: Sapir Memorial Publication Fund, 1941).

ments to represent *when*. They would speak, not of an event as an object (noun), but rather as a verb (eventing). They cannot refer spatial analogues (with a few questionable exceptions)[15] to temporal phenomena as we so readily do (e.g., a length of time, a bit of time, etc.). All of this contributes not only to their key concept of time, but even to their habits and behavior, as Whorf so admirably shows, giving to all temporal impressions the basic sense of "latering" or "eventing," which creates a fundamentally subjective, internal, and teleological time-notion. For example, the emphasis placed upon *preparation* for events clearly shows this strong sense of anticipation.[16]

In spite of the tendency toward externalized or spatialized time-concepts, however, even Indo-European has resisted the attempt to reduce time purely to a dimensional continuum, analogous to spatial dimensions. In the common speech of the average individual who speaks an Indo-European language, temporal expressions are apt to be as much fraught with feelings of desirability, of impending circumstances, of newness or age, of joy or weariness, as are forms of Athabascan, Hopi, or Bantu. For language, time has never become the mere continuum measurable according to before and after, which Aristotle defines. It has kept its original feeling of activity, even in the midst of the most abstractive tense systems. If the idea of a single, simple spatio-temporal continuum should ever so take hold of the popular conception as to rule out the aspects, we should find our language imitating our present-day physics with a single spatio-temporal continuum reflected by a new space-tense system in language. There appears to be something repellent or inherently improbable in such a development. Perhaps this is prejudice, perhaps it is the primitive intuition of the builders of our languages.

---

15. *Ibid.*, p. 84 note.
16. *Ibid.*, p. 85.

Time as Dimension and History [37

Religious and Mythological Contributions to the Time-Concept

The mythology of primitive peoples offers us their most conscious effort toward a pre-philosophical and pre-scientific explanation of the universe. Religious ritual is the result of the almost instinctive human urge to put oneself in touch with the forces and powers of this universe. It is not surpising, then, that all phases of primitive life are closely concerned with mythical interpretations and ritualistic activities.

There are certain periods during the seasonal or astronomical changes which are peculiarly marked for their religious character. Certain days, months, or years may be considered as especially sacred or holy. Frequently such periods acquire a complex of rigorous tabus, as the *dies fasti* and *nefasti* of the Romans, the Uayeb Days of the Maya, or even our own primitive *holi*-days. The sacred is thus disseminated into the calendar, sometimes dominating it, and oftentimes affording the chief reference points for calendric computations.

The philosophy of myth, usually animistic, is basically the reading of human traits into the world. At least, from our sophisticated and humanistic point of view, we seem to see these traits only as human rather than as really superhuman. (Xenophanes, c.500 B.C., was already sophisticated enough to say that if oxen had gods they would be oxen.) The world is conceived animistically as the product of forces actuated by impulses, desires, appetites, and will-power analogous to our own. These powers will not be necessarily in the human image, but they must at least possess mysterious and exalted traits. They are the dispensers of the holy and sacred character, that is, we might say the important, significant, or valuable character which is attached to the things of experience. And on the primitive level natural and human laws are not distingished, since obviously the human attitude motivates both, so that both are ascribed to the sacred power.

For illustration let us consider the Wakonda of the Omaha. Wakonda would roughly be the accumulated power of all the sacred or "wakan" character of the world. According to Miss Fletcher,[17] old men of the Omaha have said: " 'Wakonda causes day to follow night without variation [cf. Anaximander's notion that justice demands that the sun rise every day] and summer to follow winter; we can depend on these regular changes and can order our lives by them [cf. *Timaeus*, 47, wherein Plato states that God gave us sight to regard the regularities of the heavens and thereby set our own vagaries in order]. In this way Wakonda teaches us that our words and our acts must be truthful [i.e., reliable, predictable], so that we may live in peace and happiness with one another. Our fathers thought about these things and observed the acts of Wakonda, and their words have come down to us.' " Characterizing the concept of Wakonda, Miss Fletcher remarks: "Visible nature seems to have mirrored to the Omaha mind the everpresent activities of the invisible and mysterious Wakonda, and to have been an instructor in both religion and ethics."

Mythically conceived, nature, in all its aspects, including temporal ones, is the mirror of man. Cassirer has said: "The changing of day into night, the blooming and withering of the plant world, the cyclic succession of seasons: the mythological consciousness understands these phenomena at first only because it projects them on the nature of man, seeing them reflected in it as in a mirror. There arises in this reciprocal relation a mythological time-sense, which forms the bridge between the subjective life-form and the objective intuition of nature."[18] The objective is understood insofar as it picks up and reflects human nature, and man finds himself significant to the extent that his own traits

---

17. Fletcher and LaFlesche, "The Omaha Tribe," *27th Annual Report*. BAE, p. 598.
18. Cassirer, *op. cit.*, Vol. II, p. 139.

are thus reflected: he sees himself in the world, and he sees the world in himself.

In treating of the concept of time in religion and mythology, MM. Hubert and Mauss[19] distinguish between rhythm which is the internal pulsation of human life, especially group life, and simple, quantitatively measured periods. Measured equivalences are not important from the sacred and religious point of view, but recurrent rhythm of certain sacred qualities is very important. Qualitative equivalences, they maintain, are due to the peculiar sacred quality or mythological meaning which surrounds certain rites, and not to the intervals which elapse between these rites. Hubert and Mauss believe, not only that this rhythm is a projection or discovery in the world of the significances of human life, but also that these significances are really felt to be the permanent, time-transcending values of the world. This is due to the fact that rituals commemorate events, usually of a mythologic character, which in themselves have an eternal nature. The ritual itself, however, must keep a certain amount of temporal determination, since it recurs in time, whereas the mythical events may occur outside of any human time scale, or in the total extent of time. Mythology has attempted to put these events into temporal orientation of great significance by placing them at the beginning (cosmogony) or at the end (eschatology). And cosmogonical myths often are derived from group histories (migration legends, etc.), showing again the mirroring of human life in the external world. Also eschatological myths often appear to be derived from the cosmogonic ones. The regular recurrence of rites, then, is not for the purpose of counting off periods of duration, but to preserve the eternally significant character of the events. As Hubert and Mauss remark: "For religion and magic, the calendar has for object not to measure but to rhythm time."[20] Or as we might put

---

19. *Mélanges d'histoire des religion*, (2nd ed.; Paris: Alcan, 1929), pp. 189 ff.
20. *Ibid.*, p. 195.

it, the internal character of the event commemorated is all important; the measured interval between recurrences is secondary.

Of course we are aware that numbers acquire special sacred characters, so that the length of the period as marked by a sacred number may seem to have in itself the sacred quality. But again, it is not the interval measured, but the sacred quality attaching itself to the number of intervals which makes this apparent measure significant. For example, the spatial division of the plane of the earth by the North American Indian into four quarters is endlessly reproduced in his ritual and myth. Sometimes these four directions are combined with the three vertical stages to give the significant number seven, and oftentimes various combinations of these numbers give different mystic numbers. But always it is the cosmic and transcendent significance of these numbers which makes them peculiarly valuable. The sacred number may be more ordinal than cardinal at first.[21] It may represent the pulse of life moving from stage to stage. Taking the American Indian again as example, we find a commonplace division of life into four stops or four "hills," such as infancy, youth, adulthood, and old age. With other peoples the division is often threefold instead of fourfold, but the Indian's favorite spatial number shows up here in a temporal connection. This does not necessarily indicate a direct carry-over from an external spatial concept to a temporal one, but is rather an evidence of the permeating character of the mystic number itself which has been thoroughly abstracted from its spatial meaning.[22]

The mythologic and ritualistic time-sense represents basically, then, the mirroring of human life, either individual or group life, in the world. It represents the eternalization and the giving of superhuman meaning to life and

---
21. Cf. the theory of Professor Rey already mentioned.
22. Cf. the evidence given by Whorf on the Hopi as mentioned, pp. 35f.

history. Now, in all of this the points of greatest significance are the beginning and the ending, the launching and the achieving of human or cosmic purposes. Primitive philosophy is spontaneously teleological.

Beginnings and endings, however, are by themselves only the marks of temporal *intervals,* without the qualitative character which the sacred should give to events. It is because these beginnings and endings are "critical dates," as Hubert and Mauss call them, that they are more than simple measures of temporal intervals. As critical dates they transfer the sacred quality, which they themselves possess, to the intervening period, so that the period is qualified by the critical dates from which and toward which it is moving. These critical dates are the marks of permanent and eternal qualities, so that they are in a sense identical, each one being both an end and a beginning. That is to say, the end of one period is the beginning of another similar one, and the period which is delimited by such critical dates is primarily qualified by the anticipation of a new beginning.[23]

The life-pattern is marked by a beginning and an end. It is progressive, not cyclic; that is, it goes by successive stages, not by recurrences. But with the concept of endless duration there comes the need to extend somehow the universal life-pattern into eternity. The universe may be endowed with an ultimate beginning and ending. But the human mind struggles against the final dissolution of all reality or value. Each stage of the progressive life may be endlessly prolonged. In Brahmanism, for example, four *yugas,* or ages of the world, which together constitute a period of 12,000 years, are expanded almost beyond conception by interpreting the period as referring to Divine years consisting of 360 human years, so that the period becomes 4,320,000 years (a *mahayuga*). At first this represented the length of time from a creation to a destruction; but

---

23. E.g., the Aztec fifty-two year cycle.

the period became lengthened again to a *kalpa,* or a thousand of these periods (*mahayugas*). In spite of the notion of destiny underlying this progression, the feeling of endless process triumphs, leading to a definitely cyclic concept, which many peoples seem to prefer in dealing with such frankly unsatisfactory ideas. Calendric recurrences naturally support the recurrent or cyclic pattern. The character of the intervening period lessens and the sense of mere repetition increases. Each period, in the extreme, is an exact repetition of itself (as with the Stoic notion where a periodic *ekpyrosis* or universal conflagration marks the end and beginning of each identical cycle). Usually subsequent periods are in most respects alike, yet with possible differences (an effort toward compromise). Within itself the period may be entirely progressive, marked by the symbolism of the stages of life. Or the period may have the astonishing character of reversing this progression. Probably the most striking case of this latter is the Buddhist extension of the Brahmanist notions mentioned above. The Buddhists reversed the four successive *yugas* after each fulfilled period, so that events were retraced in reverse order. This Buddhist concept is elaborated almost to the ridiculous by the Jains, who liken time to a wheel with twelve spokes, six of which are passed in the ascent and six in the descent. While ascending, everything increases, the length of the periods themselves increases, and the size of all things; whereas in the descending period it all decreases again. This is not a truly wheel-like image, but resembles more the process of expansion and contraction suggested also by Anaximenes and Empedocles, and which more probably takes its real image from the process of breathing.[24]

---

24. Cf. Jacobi, "Ages of the World (Indian)," *Encyclopedia of Religion and Ethics,* James Hastings, editor (N. Y.: Charles Scribner's Sons, 1908), vol. I, pp. 200 ff. "The Jainas liken time to a wheel with twelve spokes: the descending half of the wheel is called the *avasarpini,* ... divided into six Ages (ara = spoke). The *aras* are, in avasarpini, the following: (1) susamasusama, the duration of which

TIME AS DIMENSION AND HISTORY [43

Let us assume, with Hubert and Mauss, that the critical dates which mark the beginnings and endings of periods are qualitatively identical, and that they disseminate the eternally valuable qualities of the universe into the time stream. The chief significance, then, of these critical dates will be their value as points of contact with a superior order of reality. Now it may be that each critical date represents an equivalent opportunity to make such contact, or it may

---

is 400,000,000,000,000 oceans of years; (2) susama, 300 billions of oceans of years; (3) susamadusama, 200 billions of oceans of years; (4) dusamasusama, 100 billions of oceans of years, less 42,000 common years; (5) dusama, 21,000 years; (6) dusama-dusama, likewise 21,000 years. The same Ages recur in the utsarpini period [the ascending half of the wheel], but in reversed order."

Cf. also Smith, "Ages of the World (Greek)," *Encyclopedia of Religion and Ethics*, Vol. I, p. 197-199. "The Cyclic Theory of the Ages was founded on the belief that, after the analogy of day and night, of the waxing and waning of the moon, and of the eternal round of the season, the entire Universe itself is subject to an ever-recurring cycle of change. This ancient Babylonian doctrine of the world-year, the *magnus annus*, as it was called by the Romans, makes its earliest appearance on Greek soil with Heraclitus, was thoroughly discussed by the later philosophers, and finally became known to the world at large. . . . The association of this idea with the old folk-legend of the Ages was inevitable, and appears very early in Greek speculative thought." This *magnus annus*, according to Plato's definition, is "the period which elapses before the eight circles of the planets, each revolving about the earth in an orbit of its own, arrive simultaneously at the point from which they started at the beginning of our cycle." It was believed by some, we may note, that in the following period there was a counter revolution during which time everything happened in reverse order. Men were born from the earth (*autochthones*) as old men and disappeared as infants. Hesiod seems to have had this belief in mind when he said: "This race shall Zeus destroy when men are born with hoary hair." *Works and Days*, 180-1.

Smith tells us also that "the cycle of the Universe had been called a year. This led to the natural but quite illogical assumption that, for that very reason, it must necessarily possess all the attributes of its prototype and namesake, the solar year. Second, the present condition of the world depends upon the maintenance of the elements in a certain state of equilibrium. Any disturbance of it is at once reflected in the world about us. If the disturbance is sufficiently severe, the result is cosmic disaster. The character of the disaster is determined by whichever one of the elements has gained the upper hand. Finally, great significance was attached to the fact that there were four Elements, four Seasons, four Ages of man." The story of the deluge was combined with the older Stoic conflagration, so that Cicero and Seneca knew the story as an alternation of two different destructions, a destruction by fire in the summer of the Great Year, and a destruction by water in winter. It was left only to introduce earth and air in order to have the four elements of the Greek cosmos. This was done in certain later schools by connecting them with the Four Ages. The Golden Age is dominated by fire, the Silver Age by air, the Bronze Age by water, and the Iron Age by earth. Teleologically this doctrine took the form of the fall of man due to his ever-increasing removal from the Divine Fire of the Golden Age.

be that there is a cumulative effect which gives greater value to later points, or the opposite. There is a noticeable tendency on the part of mythologies to ascribe an increasing or decreasing order of value to successive ages or stages. The four periods of a human life are likely to be marked by increasing communion with the spirit powers, until the old men have a peculiarly close contact. In the idea of transmigration there is the possibility of improving one's lot in a later incarnation. On the other hand, Greek mythology ascribes to world history the opposite course in its notion of the descent from the golden age. The realizing or losing of the eternal values, then, must also be considered. But let it be noted, there is more moral efficacy in a doctrine which allows for a change in the eternal values touched than there is in one in which these values are left always the same. Now, the completely cyclic patterns (as the Stoic, Buddhist, etc.), while allowing for a change of value within a period, can never promise any ultimate improvement, unless one resort to a Buddhist escape from the endlessly recurring process. So it would appear in general that the cyclic concept is not entirely compatible with the religious and mythological need for a transcendent value order. This may explain, in part, why the religions which believe in such cycles are apt to be pessimistic.

Cosmogonical myths, extending the life-pattern of man to the universe, were ever being perplexed with the questions of that which was before creation and that which will be after annihilation. The cycle came as the gift of calendric and astronomical knowledge to aid myth in its attempt to measure the eternal. It offered itself as a unit which could be more readily grasped than the notion of endless duration; for it is closer to the forms and sizes with which man is familiar. But as a mere unit to be added and multiplied, it is not sufficient to the purposes of myth. The ethical and teleological meaning must be preserved, and this the unit alone cannot do.

CHAPTER III

TEMPORAL DUALISM IN GREEK PHILOSOPHY

In the distinctive development of abstract thought by the early Greek philosophers, two basic concepts appear. The one is that of stuff or permanent being. The other is that of change or becoming. When completely abstracted from each other and asserted to be real, these concepts were hostile. Two extremes of Greek philosophy were thus created: one, the Heraclitean doctrine of flux, the other, the Parmenidean doctrine of permanence. In their extreme forms, the Heraclitean view denies recurrence or sameness, as in the Cratylean *reductio ad absurdum;*[1] while the Parmenidean view denies change or novelty, as presumably argued in the paradoxes of Zeno. If, however, one stops short of these extremes, it is to be noted that the Heraclitean view requires a certain pattern of recurrence or sameness. Heraclitus himself identified his alternative movements, so that hot and cold, or up and down, or wet and dry, were said to be the same. This identification indicates that his flux was not complete, but implicitly contained an underlying permanent substratum which alternately became one thing and then its opposite. Incidentally, not only will stopping short of complete flux necessitate some permanence, even if it is only a pattern of repetitions or alternations, but also stopping short of Parmenidean changelessness will force one to imagine some modicum of impermanence or novelty. Thus, we observe how at the very outset of Greek philosophy the problem of sameness and novelty, of permanence and change, gives rise to a conflict which revolves around the two temporal patterns of recurrence and directionality.

The search for patterns of change, for what we should call "natural laws," lies at the very heart of the Greek in-

---
1. See Aristotle, *Metaphysics*, 1010a.

tellectual enterprise, just as it lies at the heart of modern science. These patterns of change, cycles, recurrences, of one type or another were for the Greek mind a characteristic of the intelligible and rational aspect of the cosmos. This, however, as we shall see, is not to say that all regularities or patterns were for them rational, but only that the rational was necessarily patterned.

Fate, Destiny, Necessity—whatever we may call it—was frequently for the Greek a force which maintained irrational and unintelligible patterns. Perhaps we can trace this notion back to the science and religion of the Chaldeans and Babylonians. Certainly fatalism is strong among Semitic peoples; and it seems likely that the Babylonian interest in astronomy and astrology intensified the feeling among these people that the universe was enmeshed in inflexibly fated patterns.[2] And this feeling apparently conflicted with a belief in divine intervention, which was also strongly maintained. But what is more important, both the inexorable movements of the stars and the sporadic interventions of God were inscrutable to man; he could only observe and foretell, he could not ask the reason why.

Something of this same inscrutable, and hence unintelligible or irrational, fatalism is to be found among the early Greek thinkers. According to Anaximander, we remember, the pattern of change is a separating or differentiating of opposites out of the Boundless into which they return when destroyed, and all this activity takes place *"as destiny orders."* Destiny is here a sort of police force, maintaining universal order; for it is linked immediately with justice.[3] Professor Cornford has admirably indicated the underlying connection between this apparent confusion of moral and natural law in early Greek thought through the primitive religious concept of *Moira* or *fate*. *Moira* controls even the

---

2. See especially Franz Cumont, *Astrology and Religion among the Greeks and Romans*, (New York: Putnam's, 1912).

3. See F. M. Cornford, *From Religion to Philosophy* (New York: Longmans, Green, & Co., 1912), Chapter I.

Gods in the Homeric poems. It is a "blind, automatic force" which keeps gods and natural phenomena alike within their proper bounds, punishing them the moment they transgress those bounds.[4] Professor Cornford points out further that *Moira* is beginning to be superseded in the Homeric poems by the will of Zeus, Destiny of God, etc. Now this transference of power is also reflected in Greek philosophy in the change from an irrational and blind Fate to a controlling Reason, as in the cosmology of Anaxagoras. This change is of the utmost importance to Greek thought in general.[5] It is the mark of that deep-seated Greek hope which believes that the cosmos is ultimately intelligible, organized according to patterns for which there are understandable explanations and reasons. Herein lies a fundamental difference between the Greek and the Semitic temperament: the former is convinced that there are intelligible patterns of which the human mind may know the cause or reason, the latter stands by the original inscrutability and blindness both of routine behavior and Divine intervention. Hebrew and Arabic literature resounds with the inscrutability of the ways of God and the supremacy of His Will. According to it we may know the decrees of God, but we may not question them. Greek determinism is hopeful from the point of view of human knowledge, Semitic fatalism is not.

We have then a new conflict within Greek thought, the conflict between irrational and rational pattern. This antithesis, though subtler and less obvious than that of being and becoming, is equally significant to an understanding of the Greek notions of time. It follows that cycles of themselves are not necessarily intelligible, but cycles which permit also of a *directional* movement from irrational to rational, that is, from bad to good, or even vice versa, incorporate a new feature which makes them intelligible. It

---

4. *Ibid.*, p. 20. Cf. Heracleitus, frag. 94 (Diels), in which the sun is constrained by the Erinyes, the handmaidens of Justice.

5. In this connection it is interesting to note that Thucydides blamed the Peloponnesian War on lack of Reason.

may be argued that this new feature is essentially directional and not cyclical at all, though it is of course impossible to divorce completely the cyclical and the directional.

In the Platonic dialogue, *Phaedo*, at least two important clues may be found. The first comes from the passage in which Socrates is criticizing the naturalism of Anaxagoras; for though Anaxagoras spoke of Mind or Reason as the arranger of all, he did not, as Socrates thought he should, go on to show that Mind arranges things for the best. That is, Anaxagoras gave only the disposition of things, and though he mentions an intelligence as organizing force, he does not give the *reasons* why things are arranged as they are—or, as it is put in the dialogue, he confuses the condition with the true cause.

In this criticism we notice the Greek predilection for rational explanations. We notice also the way in which a moral quality (best) is linked by means of divine intelligence and benevolence to a rational arrangement of the cosmos. That is to say, *true rational pattern requires a moral explanation*, and not a merely physical one.

In another part of the *Phaedo*, Socrates is discussing the Pythagorean doctrine of transmigration to which he appeals in support of immortality. The idea of the argument depends upon a belief in a cyclical process of coming into being and going out of being, of an alternation between life and death; for as souls are born, others must leave to maintain the balance, and the process of dying is in turn repaid by a process of rebirth. If this process were not circular in this fashion, there might come a day when all would reach the same state and the process of becoming would be at an end. Hence, arises the need for rebirth. (This discussion is very reminiscent of a modern one concerning the theory of entropy.) The concept of a cycle of births and rebirths is indeed very primitive, being a natural explanation if one considers the quantity of souls as limited. However, it is irrational and fated unless some directional character is inserted to break the automatic repetitions. Escape from the cycle of rebirths gave to the Hindus their primary notion of Heaven, and in the Myth of Er we shall have occasion to discover the Platonic (or Pythagorean) suggestion of a possible escape, a moment when rational intelligence can direct an otherwise stupid process.

We find thus a cyclical and a directional pattern of intelligibility vying with each other at the very start of Greek philosophical speculation. On the one hand all change, all becoming, is a matter of alternation, of going from one condition to its opposite and back again. Nearly every early Greek philosopher had an answer to three major problems: (1) of what stuff or elements is the Cosmos composed; (2) what forces motivate it; and (3) *what is the pattern of change*. The cosmology of Empedocles is typical. He names the primitive stuff as the four elements: earth, air, fire, and water. The forces he calls "Love" and "Hate," and the pattern of change is an *alternation* of these forces, with opposite effects. The Pythagoreans with their primary interest in arithmetic and geometry contributed strongly to this emphasis upon alternation and cycles; for repetition, let us remember, is implied in any counting or numbering, temporal or otherwise.

On the other hand, however, we must not lose sight of the tradition of directionality which is present in Greek philosophy as much as in the mythology. Cycles of alternation have goals within each stage of the movement. Also, cycles may form part of a larger process which is itself directed toward some goal. Tales of decreasing value, such as the Hesiodic myth of the descending ages of man (the Gold Age, Silver Age, Bronze Age, and Iron Age), indicate this character. And of course any series of cycles which are improved, or broken by the activity of reason, or move toward rational perfection, as intimated in the philosophy of Plato, are oriented more by the goal than by the cycle.

Nevertheless, Greek thought remains throughout more cyclical than directional in its primary emphasis.

PLATO

Plato's Theory of Ideas may be regarded as his solution of the problem of change and permanence. For Plato, the rational pattern is the permanent, and hence, in a sense, the real. The world of material mixtures is the realm of the changing. Behold the image of creation in the *Timaeus!* God looked at the *ideal pattern* and created the world; but "the nature of the ideal being was everlasting, and to bestow this attribute in its fullness upon a creature was impossible. Wherefore, he resolved to have a moving image of eternity, and when he set in order the heaven, he made this eternal image but moving according to number, while eternity rests in unity; and this image we call time."[6] It is here in this description of creation that Plato has defined time as *the moving image of eternity*, moving according to number. Eternity means unity and permanence, hence, being. There is no change in connection with it. But in the world there is change and this change is either cyclical or directional. If change is to be plotted or measured, it must be regular and recurrent, i. e., cyclical. The most perfect regular and recurrent movement is time, which moves "according to number." Eternity is completely permanent, unchanging, and timeless; so that time can only be a moving *image* of eternity.

Thus we see that the timeless eternity of Greek philosophy is really an abstraction from the cyclical time pattern, or regular recurrent movement, from which the last vestige of directionality or novelty has been removed. In eternity, the recurrences are completely identified, and all change is made impossible.

But the Platonic Ideas represent not only numerical unification (the One), but also ethical ideals (the Good). Plato was concerned, that is, with the ideal pattern in the

---

6. *Timaeus*. 37. Jowett translation (N. Y.: Random House, 1937), Vol. 2, p. 19.

sense of that which is best, as well as in the sense of that which is quantitatively measurable. The Ideas are perfect not only in the sense in which geometrical figures are perfect, but also in the sense in which complete goodness is called perfection. In fact, from many points of view the Socratic in Plato's philosophy is more prominent than the Pythagorean. The ethical ideal is typified by the *Republic*, in which the ideal state is "a pattern laid up in heaven," to guide the actions of those on earth whether they ever succeed in copying it exactly or not. There are many indications that Plato realized full well that a changeless pattern is never going to appear in the phenomenal world, doomed as the latter is to change and time. If perfection were ever achieved on earth, the necessity for change would cause its immediate relinquishment which could only be for the worse.

According to Timaeus, God in his goodness wished to make a world as good as possible, so he brought order out of disorder "considering that this was in every way better than the other."[7] But God could not make the world perfect. The pre-existing chaos, disorderly and irrational as it was, could not be rid of its material element and suddenly transformed into the perfection of a world of Ideas. God caused the material world to strive to imitate the perfection of the latter; more than this he could not do. However, we must not forget that the dynamic world is as essential to Platonism as is the world of Ideas; for either one by itself is empty and meaningless. That is, the material world must not be taken as unreal in true Platonism. Moreover, the phenomenal world is not all matter. It contains soul or spirit, and in this soul is a Godgiven drive or Eros motive toward the Good. The individual soul, replica of the divine, is ever seeking to bring more perfection and intelligibility into matter. Yet such is the nature of matter that true perfection is unattainable for it, thus dooming the Platonic world to endless activity, to ceaseless striving, and for this, *time* is the

---

7. *Timaeus*, 30.

penalty. The significance of time in Platonism is thus twofold. First, it is the image of an eternal geometric pattern, moving according to regular repetitions, that is, number. Second, time is the penalty for an endless striving toward perfection. In both cases the ideal pattern is beyond time, but especially in the latter case the meaning of the timeless pattern is as nothing without the process of striving and accomplishing which is temporal.

The directional idea is well illustrated in two of Plato's "myths." First, in the Myth of Er, we recall that the souls awaiting rebirth came to the place of the three Fates, Daughters of Necessity, where one can see how the whole planetary system is being revolved on the "spindle of Necessity." There, a prophet speaks to the souls bidding them choose according to their own preference whatever type of life they desire from among an assortment which includes animals or humans, tyrants or beggars, etc. At the moment of choice the experience and intelligence of each soul has an opportunity to assert itself, and to lead the individual to a better or worse situation. When the choice has been made, the souls pass to Lachesis who bestows upon each a genius as guardian, then to Clotho who pulls them into the revolution of the spindle, ratifying the destiny of each, and thence to Atropos who spins the threads and makes them irreversible, and without looking back they must pass beneath the throne of Necessity. From there they go to drink of Lethe, River of Forgetfulness, and finally to their rebirth into the world to be whatever they have chosen. The journey endures a thousand years, we are told.

We have here an image, distinctly Pythagorean in character, of souls guided by their own chosen destiny. There is a great cycle of a thousand years through which the souls must pass to each rebirth. At one small point in that period there is a chance for intelligence to operate, a chance for the soul to improve its future status. At this moment the irrational cycle of Fate is broken, and a directing intelligence comes into play. Clearly portrayed in this myth is the antithesis between the unintelligent and fatalistic routine of mere repetition, and the eternal instant when reason has full sway and an intelligent choice can be made.[8]

The other instructive myth for our purpose is the one in the *Statesman*. According to this myth there is a Hindu-like reversal of direction at the end of each cycle, the old story of the Earth-Born men being explained as belonging to the previous period when men were born from the earth as old men and grew younger. The Sun and Moon rose in the west instead of the east, and the whole universe rotated in the opposite direction. During this period, represented by the Age of Cronos, God controlled the cosmos and regulated its movements, but when the reversal occurred, God released the helm and the universal creature "having originally received intelligence from its author and creator, turned about and by an inherent necessity revolved in the opposite direction." This introduces the new period, the Age of Zeus, when things are left to themselves and they get worse and worse until finally the Creator again must take the helm and restore order.[9]

This story of the day when, in the Age of Cronos, life ran in reverse fashion, with God at the helm, must not be taken too seriously, Professor Taylor tells us.[10] What is significant is that the world is likened to a ship which tacks back and forth, now with an intelligent helmsman, now with none at all, except innate tendency. Or perhaps a better image is that of a revolving pendulum, which turns for a while in one direction until it has completed its course and then revolves in the other. At any rate, the time-pattern in this myth, it will be seen, is different from that of the Myth of Er, where there was no reversal of movement, nor any special period of intelligent guidance to be followed by a

---

8. This is of course a common notion in myth and ritual. See pp. 39 ff.
9. *Statesman*, 268 ff.
10. A. E. Taylor, *Plato, the Man and his Works* (3rd ed., London: Methuen and Co., Ltd., 1929), pp. 395 ff. Esp. note p. 397.

period of undoing. The Myth of Er is represented more by the image of a clock which runs from twelve to twelve, and at one point in the process intelligence is allowed to put in its oar.

In both myths we find combinations of cyclical and directonal time-patterns. Pure duration is implied as the penalty of an imperfect, mutable world. But upon this base of duration the time-patterns are superimposed. In the Myth of Er, the great cycle idea if taken purely by itself would lead one to the notion of exactly repeated event series. This is not the case, however, for each successive age is new, the preceding one being merely forgotten. Also the directional character is implied by the description of events as always moving in the same direction, as in a clock-wise movement. In the *Statesman* myth, the directional character is even further repudiated by the notion that events may proceed forwards or backwards. Nevertheless, within each period, there is a directional character implied in the moving towards or away from intelligent rule. Indeed, the reversal of events, as Professor Taylor suggests, may only be a humorous way of indicating the great difference between an age governed by intelligence and an age not so controlled. Plato, it seems, wished to indicate how dissimilar our world is from one directly controlled by God. It is, however, interesting to find a time-pattern like that of a revolving pendulum which after a number of reversals would lose any directional significance. This well illustrates the absurdity of applying a purely cyclical time-image to a life-pattern, an image wherein all events go back and forth, doing and undoing, and getting nowhere. Human life, even for Plato, is not like that. A certain amount of realization of goals and fulfillment of desires is implied in the final release of the most intelligent spirits into the world of pure souls, as intimated in the Myth of Er. There the directional time-pattern triumphs. In Platonism, complete wisdom and intelligence operate both as goal and as the means of final release which allows the soul to attain this goal.

But Plato was still too near the geometrical ideal to realize a definite directional time-pattern as paramount. For him, the ideal is limited and patterned, balanced and symmetrical, like the forms of the geometers. This ideal carries us into a world of perfect patterns, particularly circles, which are really motionless cycles. So, in escaping from the world of changing cycles, through the directional effort of realizing perfect understanding, we come into a world of changeless cycles. The patterned and measured are still with us. The value quality of the intelligent, that is, the Good, is in a sense subservient to the One.

Time is the "moving image of eternity," moving according to a measurable pattern. This definition agrees with Plato's ideal of intelligibility, linked as that is with the geometrical and numberable. But it is significant that it is the effort to apply number and pattern to the phenomenal world, the effort, that is, to realize greater meaning and intelligibility in connection with a moving and dynamic world, which gives to Plato's philosophy a valuational and ethical character. Without the implication of this directional time-pattern, therefore, the world of pure forms would be as meaninglessly aloof as Aristotle seemed to consider it.

ARISTOTLE

Of all Greek philosophers, it was perhaps Aristotle whose philosophy held more promise for a preëminently directional time-pattern. His early interest in biology and growth led him to the necessary insight for distinguishing the directional pattern in the world of living organisms from the more purely geometrical pattern of a physical and astronomical universe. Nonetheless, Aristotle was too catholic in his interests to neglect the physical point of view, and too Greek to give it a genuinely subordinate position. In his *Physics* the discussion of time is primarily concerned with measurement. It is in his *Metaphysics*, with the discussion of potentiality, that the directional time-pattern comes into prominence. In the end, Aristotle is faced with a profound dilemma; for he must select a universe which is ultimately dynamic or one which is static, one which is a series of novelties or one which is only a series of repetitions. Is actuality really the activity which the word implies;[11] or is it an unchanging substratum? Is the Divine Ruler of the Cosmos an active motivator, or an almost static changeless mover? Is there real evolution in the world, or is there just a recurrence of certain event patterns? It is difficult to find a satisfactory solution to these questions, and it may very well be that Aristotle was perplexed by them to the end.

The most striking feature of Aristotle's treatment of the nature of time in the *Physics* is his effort to base it upon the concept of a continuum. The temporal continuum, be it noted, is no different from the spatial continuum, save for its unidirectional character. Whereas the spatial continuum may be measured in any direction from the here-point, the temporal continuum is defined by the continuous movement of the now-point always from before to after. In Aristotle's full definition, time is the number (measure) of movement according to before and after, that is, measurable by reason of the before-after relation of successive now-points.[12] How much of a directional character of time is implied in this definition? So far as mere measurability is concerned, it is conceivable that the temporal continuum could be measured equally well by a succession of now-points from before to after or from after to before, just as the spatial continuum could be measured from here to there or from there to here. Thus, for purposes of measurement, direction is immaterial. Yet Aristotle insists upon the unidirectionality of the temporal continuum, implying as an

---

11. The Greek word *energeia* is used both for activity and actuality.
12. See *Physics*, 219b and 220a.

Time as Dimension and History

essential time-trait that the measuring should be always in the same direction.

The real difficulty with the Aristotelian definition of time arises, however, when we ask ourselves how time is a measuring. For measurement of a continuum necessitates a series of regularly marked off and equal intervals, that is, some kind of regular discreteness. Aristotle seemed to think that the now-point might serve as that which marks off successive intervals, so he asks the question: Is the now the same throughout or is it different? Typically, he answers that in a sense it is and in a sense it is not. It depends on how we think of it. If we abstract the now-point from the continuum, it is obviously the same; but if we think of it as moving along the continuum it is analogous to the moving object in that it is always entering into new relations with its surroundings, thus continuously acquiring a certain novelty. But in either case the now-point contributes no regular discreteness and is therefore not a very satisfactory basis for the numbering of the temporal continuum. Aristotle's efforts to press it into such service prove rather futile. The best he can do is to insist that, though the now-point is not a part of the temporal continuum, it is a necessary attribute of time which serves as boundary between any successive parts of the continuum. The difficulty is, of course, that there is no set of discrete now-points, like railroad ties, to be passed over as time goes on, but rather that the now-point itself is thought of as moving along like the train. Also, having defined a continuum as that which is potentially divisible at any point, Aristotle has eliminated any possibility of finding discreteness, and hence of finding a basis of measure *within* the continuum itself.

If time were defined as a kind of recurrent movement, it would have within it the basis for measure. Aristotle has ruled, however, that time is not change, not a kind of movement, but a sort of scale by which movement can be numerically estimated. Thus, the source of the numbering is thrust squarely on the shoulders of time. To be sure, he says that time and change are mutually interdependent, but he realizes that rest also takes time and that accelerations or decelerations do not alter the amount of time, so he makes time simply the basis for measuring change or rest. To be in time is defined as being measured by time. Eternally unchanging things or non-existent things, he claims, are not in time.

As a sort of inspiration, Aristotle distinguishes two meanings of number: that which we count and that by which we count. Time is the former, not the latter. In other words, it is not a series of abstract numbers, but something to which those numbers are applicable. He thus seems to reiterate that there is something in the nature of time itself which makes it measurable. But we are still at a loss for that quality of time which actually enables it to be counted. And the best we can do is to say that "time is not movement, but only movement in so far as it admits of enumeration,"[13] that is, it is the abstracted numerability of movement, which is little more than a reiteration of the first definition.

Aristotle is reduced to seeking the basis for measuring movement itself. He recognizes that this measure which is temporal measure should apply equally to any of the four types of change (i. e., generation and destruction, qualitative change, quantitative change, or locomotion).[14] But when it comes to the selection of the most regular type of change, as the one most suitable for giving discreteness to the temporal continuum, Aristotle rejects alteration (change of quality), increase (change of quantity), and growth and decay, and settles upon circular locomotion. Of course, he has in mind the diurnal rotation, the annual recurrence of seasons, and all regularly recurrent phenomena. It is because of the necessity of measuring time by such phenomena, Aristotle re-

---
13. *Ibid.*, 219b.
14. *Ibid.*, 223a 30-35.

marks, that people are in the habit of thinking of all human affairs as cyclical, even life and death, generation and destruction. "This is because all of these things are distinguished in time, and realize their ends and their beginnings as if according to some period; for time itself is deemed to be a sort of cycle."[15]

Thus a continuous cyclical movement is adopted as best representing the time-pattern. The directional character is still faintly suggested by the fact that a circular movement is at least not reversible, but continues in one direction, e. g., clockwise. A natural division or discreteness is given by the recurrent nature of the movement, and when this movement is cosmic, as in the case of the diurnal rotation, which the Greeks thought to be a rotation of the celestial sphere, the Greek faith in cosmic perfection would seem to assure the equality of succeeding intervals. Some such faith is necessary to temporal measurement. So Aristotle's struggle to find the basis of measurability as somehow within the nature of time, or as constituting its essence, ends in the faith that somewhere in the world of movement will be found the needed discreteness. His initial hope has proven vain, for he has had to go outside the nature of time, as he defined it, to find that very basis of measurement which he had made a part of its essence.

However, the great lack in the image of the recurrent cycle is that of genuine novelty or accumulation, for this is a trait which is essential to a directional time-pattern. If it is neglected, time itself will become nothing but a series of absolute recurrences in which the events of one cycle are indistinguishable from those of another. Such a time-pattern will not accord with the growth pattern, which is Aristotle's great image in the *Metaphysics*, Book Theta. His biological preconceptions reassert themselves, and in dealing with genesis and potentiality he dwells upon a growth pat-

---

15. *Ibid.*, 223b 27-29. (Cf. *Meta.* 1071b 2-11, *De Gen*, II, 11, and *Meteores*, I, 2.)

tern which is to be understood much more definitely in terms of a directional becoming from that which is to that which is not, i. e., to that which exists in fictive or potential time. In the growth pattern the progressive and cumulative character of the process is assured. There is no mere repetition. The explanation of potentiality is in terms of entire processes which lead from something to something else, and which are therefore just the antithesis of circular locomotions.

Aristotle takes it as axiomatic that nothing can come from nothing, and that some actual reality must be present before evolutions are possible. This of course does not mean that the process somehow must be completely actual in advance. It was from this absurd supposition, Aristotle notes, that the sophistic quibble arose which claims that one cannot learn unless one already possesses the knowledge, in which case it is not learning. Aristotle replies,[16] "of that which is coming to be, some part must have come to be, . . . and he who is learning must, it would seem, possess some part of the science." Actuality is thus both prior and posterior in time to potentiality. That is, actuality plus potentiality produces *new* actuality, whether it is a process of learning or begetting. In the growth process, the actuality of the future man is potentially in the child but the actuality of the child must precede and the actuality of the parent is prior to the child. The initial actuality is in a sense fragmentary from the point of view of the final actuality, thus emphasizing the novelty of the final actuality and the cumulative character of the process.

Growth processes, it is true, may be considered as cycles. The "cycle of life," as it is often called, occurs over and over again, and if there is no ultimate evolutionary process for reference, it might seem that these cycles are as truly repetitive as the planetary motions. If the physical characteristics

---

16. *Metaphysics*, 1049b 29 ff. (Ross translation.)

or the learning of animals is unchanging, then each successive generation merely repeats the nature and activities of its predecessors. If such were the case, the sophistic quibble would have a certain truth from the point of view of the race as a whole; for there would be nothing learned that was not already known. But Aristotle certainly considered learning and biological development more in the light of potentiality for change than in the light of such complete repetition. He hints at a biological evolution,[17] and, especially in his *Ethics*, there is at least the vision of a more completely intellectualized race, whether or not he ever anticipated that such a one would be realized on earth.

Men and animals do not return upon themselves, Aristotle tells us,[18] but new generations are composed of new individuals, even if the species remains the same. This type of process he calls a "rectilinear sequence," which is another way of saying "directional." Thus the ultimate novelty, for Aristotle, is really in terms of the individual life and not in terms of the general pattern. Starting with individuals as ultimate realities, Aristotle could not escape this realization, and the recognition of it is confirmed by the statement that the reality of the change is the changing individual, who must be new in each new life process. With the abandonment of universals as ultimate actualities, Aristotle loses Plato's sameness as the basic character of reality. To Aristotle, it is not the repetition or sameness of cycles which is important, it is the novelty within each process, it is the *entelechy*, that is, which serves as *causa explicandi*.

Activities, however, which contain their own ends, and which are therefore not potential as Aristotle has defined it, lack the directional character of potential or instrumental processes. For example, Aristotle's Contemplative Deity is

---

17. However, see the article by Harry Beal Torrey and Frances Felin, "Was Aristotle an Evolutionist?" in *The Quarterly Review of Biology*, Vol. 12, No. 1, pp. 1-18. There seems no question of Aristotle's dominating preconception of fixed species.
18. *De Gen., et Corrup.*, 338 b .

engaged in the intrinsic process of rational activity. He has nothing potential about him, and hence no basis for accomplishment or novelty, or even for change, though he is said to be active. There is in this respect more of a static nature in Aristotle's Divinity than in Plato's Demiurge. Completely actual processes of this kind are really more akin to a perfect circular movement than to a directional time-pattern.

Substratum, as primary matter, likewise, though transformable even in its essential traits through generation and corruption, is in itself perfectly static, conserved throughout the universe just as surely as is energy according to a more modern hypothesis. Thus in Aristotelianism the only kind of truly directional change occurs in the fulfillment of potentiality.

Nonetheless, the surprising thing is not how little but how much Aristotle devotes to the idea of potentiality. In spite of the Greek axiom that nothing can come from nothing, in spite of the Platonic emphasis on sameness and eternal pattern, Aristotle appreciates the reality of genetic processes and hence of that sort of change which produces novelty, which has a beginning and an ending and a directional frame of reference. The emphasis on the reality of the individual, and his anti-Platonic attack on the reality of the archetype led him to the recognition of novelty within each new fulfillment of a potentiality, even when repeating a given growth pattern. We must not forget that it is the changing, moving individual which remains the primary reality of the Aristotelian cosmos.

It is Aristotle's great dilemma that this individual substance is indescribable except in terms of general characteristics. The pattern of change, the final form, the type of matter, the moving force—all these may remain the same for different cases. These are the generalities; and these are certainly for Aristotle the bases of all explanation. It must be acceded that if these formal, final, material, and efficient attributes of individual substances remain ultimately unchanging, then Aristotle has no real cosmic novelty. His universe will be as static as that of Plato. And macroscopically, this appears to be the case. Substratum is conserved. God is either an unchanging process of self-contemplative reason, or, as Prime Mover, a sort of a magnetic attraction, inactive himself. The real motivation is not so much in God as in the world itself, in its desire for perfection. Like the Eros motive of Plato's world, it is within the individual substance that the desire or tendency is to be found which carries it onward to the fulfillment of potentialities, and to the accomplishment of divine purpose.

Macroscopically the universe appears static; microscopically it is composed of individuals acting directionally. In the large, the processes are already perfect—like the circular movements of the sphere, or the reasonings of God. In the minute, there are real accomplishments. Between these two world views, both present in Aristotelianism, there seems to be as much of a gulf as there is between Aristotle's celestial and sub-lunar spheres. Which is the true world? In his more anti-Platonic moments, Aristotle apparently favors the microscopic world, the world of individual substances. At other times, he seems to see only substratum and God, his two great eternals.

The two time-patterns are here shown in cosmic conflict. On the one hand there is perfect circularity, easily measured, an unending series of finite events, the limits of which are all-important, the content of which is nothing. Even a cumulation of numbers is meaningless when it has no beginning and stretches onward infinitely toward no goal. Direction here has lost the frame of reference which would give it meaning. On the other hand, where there is potentiality and motivation, we have a beginning and an ending, a pattern of progression and a final form toward which it moves. The time-pattern is not here the numbering of movement according to before and after; it is the direction of movement from beginning to end. It is not the counting of equal finite events repeated over and over; it is the course of cumulative and novel events within the process. It is not an explanation of time based on measurement; but an explanation of time based on accomplishment of value.

We might point out, finally, that Aristotle's "before" and "after" are not capable of being known in any other way than as representing a tendency from something and toward something. Hence, we could conclude that his real time determiner is the *entelechal* process, being the fulfillment of a potential end-form, and neither a measurable movement of a now-point from before to after nor a succession of nows.

POST-ARISTOTELIAN SUGGESTIONS

After Aristotle, the Peripatetics were left with the problem of the nature of the fundamental movement of which time is the measure, and how a measurable discreteness can be found in the nature of time. Straton saw clearly that Aristotle's quest for such discreteness within the nature of time itself had been vain; so he brought the emphasis back to the continuity of time, making time the concomitant of events and the basis for comparing their rate. Thus, time is still considered as a form of measure, but a measure based on the relativity of movements rather than upon an intrinsic numbering.

For Neoplatonism, however, time was not conceived as relative to the movements of the sensible world, but as itself an absolute movement in the World-Soul. This primordial time in the Soul becomes the cause and ground of the physical Aristotelian time. Neoplatonic metaphysics was concerned with the relation of the Intelligence to the Soul. The former was thought of as the eternal ground of the universe, while the latter was mobile and living, though immortal. According to Plotinus, there is no time for *Nous* (Intelligence), which is immobile and timeless, but the primordial time is in the World-Soul, and this primordial time is the "image of eternity" of the Platonic definition. However, the phrase has even greater emphasis here, since there is new importance attached to the eternal. Man cannot measure time, but a measure of movement will give him an idea of the nature of time; for it is with the aid of the visible that we measure the invisible.[19]

Thus, after Aristotle, the problem of the measurement of time was referred back to a non-numerical, more subjective, comparison of actions and movements by Aristotle's own followers, the Peripatetics; while the Neoplatonists sought the basis of measurement in the movement of the Soul which underlies all cosmic motions. For both of these groups, the eternal is of a nature different from the temporal. Yet the two are linked together by means of cycles and recurring epochs which seemed to them to possess some of the character of both eternity and time.

Greek thought is characterized by the effort to apply measurement wherever possible. But before one can measure, one must have the means wherewith to count. One must have a unit and a point of departure or reference. In dealing with time, the Greeks were seeking both a unit of measure and also a metaphysical frame of reference in which this unit would have meaning. The concept of cycle or recurrence remains on the whole dominant throughout Greek thought as that which best satisfies the needed condition of temporal intelligibility. The continuum can be measured by cycles, and events can be arranged in general patterns of recurrence. The cycle is always the "image of eternity," for it can be represented geometrically by the circle, and this was for the Greek a most perfect and eternal pattern.

---

19. *Enneads*, III, Bk. vii, ch. xi. See Duhem, *Système du Monde* (Paris: A. Hermann et fils, 1913), Vol. I, p. 248.

CHAPTER IV

CHRISTIAN DRAMA AND THE RENAISSANCE OF QUANTITY

The problem of time-concepts in modern thought depends greatly upon the dichotomies of human thinking and of human interests. The central problems of the Patristic and Scholastic philosophies are other than those of Rationalists and Empiricists, or Idealists and Realists. However, the character of the problem of time, wherever met, reflects the duality of meaning which we have already analyzed.

The Greek concept of time had placed the emphasis very strongly upon the repetitive temporal image in which a sense of directionality is almost lacking. The Hindu had also encouraged a view of endless cycles in which repetitions and even reversals were commonplace. The Hebrew concept, however, was already strongly directional in character, being based on a unique creation followed by a genealogical historical procession of patriarchs, and including a teleological messianic tradition, product of a yearning for worldly strength and also supermundane bliss.

With Christianity, the notion of cosmic drama is reinforced by the crystallization of the messianic tradition in an historical event. The ancient apocalyptic prophecies are fulfilled, the drama is accomplished. As Vossler says of St. Paul, who was so peculiarly responsible for the formation of a Christian religion, "In the centre of the new religion and midway in the history of earth and eternity, he sets the cross and the resurrection. From this point all relations are measured; it separates sharply the old from the new; it sets off the thought of Israel, of Greece, of the Gospels. Adam's fall through sin becomes the first act in the drama of salvation. Through Adam, God's grace is forfeited; hereditary sin becomes dominant. Human nature must be degraded to the lowest depravity so that salvation through Christ may appear the more glorious. . . . The fall, the crucifixion, the resurrection, the last judgment, were all in God's plan from the beginning."[1]

From the point of view of the individual also, Christianity lends emphasis to the dramatic temporal image. In a very definite way the central theme of Christianity is the dramatic course of the human soul from birth to death, to the day of judgment, and to eternal salvation or damnation. The allegorical tale of the pilgrim on earth, the erring wayfarer and his succor, these constitute the fabric of Christianity much more than the refined and rational attire of universals and particulars, or more than proofs of God's existence. It may be, as Gunn says,[2] that the scholastic mind was not interested in time and space, but rather in the logic of the universe. Nevertheless, the average Christian was very much aware of his own temporal reality, and of his own prospect at the seat of judgment.

Anselm, in the *Cur Deus Homo*, touches the dramatic quality of Christianity when he falls from the formal language of his theology to explain the episode of Christ in the Christian drama more in accordance with the idiom and metaphor of the religion, by speaking in terms of "Father" and "Son" rather than in terms of the three persons of the Godhead. We seem to understand the Christian drama better when we say that "the Son freely gave himself to the Father," than when we say that God gave "his humanity to his divinity." For "by the names of Father and Son," Anselm adds, "a wondrous depth of devotion is excited in the hearts of the hearers, when it is said that the Son supplicates the Father on our behalf."[3] This dramatic Christianity has

---

1. Karl Vossler, *Medieval Culture* (New York: Harcourt, Brace, and Co., 1929), Vol. I, p. 38.
2. J. A. Gunn, *The Problem of Time* (London: Geo. Allen & Unwin, Ltd., 1929), p. 44.
3. *Cur Deus Homo*, Ch. xviii b. Translation by S. N. Deane. See also, H. B. Alexander, *God and Man's Destiny* (Oxford University Press, 1936), Chapter V.

a much more powerful appeal than the logical theology of strict Scholasticism.

The transition to a Christian concept of time is particularly noticeable in the idea of eternity. The Greek notion of a timeless eternal was in a large measure the product of the Greek preoccupation with cycles, since, as we have seen, the emphasis upon repeated cycles tends to diminish the sense of duration and to lead logically to the notion of durationless, static patterns. One is left either with almost identical repetitions or with a complete timeless permanence. For Christianity, however, eternity was neither an eternity of endless repetitions nor an eternity of the time-transcending durationless type, but rather of an endless future in which the souls born into this world may realize goods or expiate sins for the accomplishment of which a finite time would be inadequate.

This new meaning of eternity is well illustrated in the Christian doctrine of the Ages of the World. The Greek and Hindu conception of endless recurrences gives way to a single cosmic drama arranged in epochs, a world-drama which involves a beginning but no end. This is the "single cosmic drama" of Christianity, as Dean Inge so clearly describes it.[4] Saint Augustine, at the conclusion of the *City of God*, foresees this "most great Sabbath having no evening" as the seventh day, the day of eternal rest which is to come at the conclusion of six previous epochs, which were respectively: (1) from Adam to the flood, (2) from the flood to Abraham, (3) from Abraham to David, (4) from David to the Babylonian exile, (5) from then to the birth of Christ, and (6) the present, which includes all the time from the birth of Christ to the coming of the Kingdom of God. This sixth epoch, he tells us, cannot be measured in numbers of years, for it is rather the event that counts. The seventh epoch ends not in an evening, but in the Lord's day, which he

---

4. W. R. Inge, *God and the Astronomers* (Longmans Green & Co., 1933),) p. 81.

terms "the eighth eternal day." "There we shall rest, and see, and love, and praise: . . . For what other thing is our end, but to come to that kingdom of which there is no end."[5] The cosmic drama has here its final release, its exalted image of the afterlife. There is no endless counting of revolutions and cycles, but only a single triumphant climax. Nor is it the equality of temporal durations that is important, but the number of generations, and not even the number so much as the events themselves. There are analogies between human life and world history, between the ages of man and the ages of the world.

The tradition of dramatic epochs continues through Christian philosophy.[6] Erigena, for example, divided the world's history into three great epochs, placing the first five ages of Augustine in the first epoch. The second epoch of this scheme is the Christian era, and the third is the future eternity when all the faithful will serve as priests and see God face to face. For Christian thought in general, a future eternity is demanded for the realization of perfect values.

In the Thomistic synthesis of Greek and Christian thought, the logical side of Scholasticism comes to the fore, and the dramatic, though ever-present, is subordinate. St. Thomas reaffirmed the Aristotelian definition of time as the measurement of movement according to before and after, despite the fact that St. Augustine had acutely exhibited the difficulties and paradoxes which arise from an effort to define time in this manner.[7] This new emphasis upon temporal measurement and the relation of time to movement served to revive a new interest in quantitative aspects which was to flower with the Renaissance and its scientific inquiries. But St. Thomas also emphasized another sort of

---

5. Translation by John Healey. (1931 edition; London: J. M. Dent & Sons, Ltd.)
6. See G. Bonet-Maury, "Ages of the World (Christian)" in the *Encyclopaedia of Religion and Ethics*, Vol. I, p. 191.
7. See especially Augustine's queries on the reality of the past and future outside memory and expectation, and his difficulties with an instantaneous "now." *Confessions*, Bk. XI.

temporal category, namely, the timeless eternal of Greek philosophy; for, in Thomism, as indeed in all logical Scholasticism, God is qualified temporally as completely eternal, by an *aeternitas* which is also a *tota simul*, or "all things at once," which is a timeless perfection. But the most interesting and peculiarly Christian temporal category in Thomism is the endless age or *aevum* which is inserted as a sort of mean between *aeternitas* and measured, terrestrial time. This *aevum* is attributable to the pure intelligences and the disembodied souls, which, though containing potentiality, are incorruptible; for while they *can* know all things (though only through intelligible essences) they nevertheless do not know them all at once, as God does, so that in this respect at least there is an eternal activity. Thus we escape the logical predicament in which unchanging perfection is connected with an endless duration. The Greek logic which led to the only alternatives of a measured and eventful time and a timeless eternity is broken and a middle ground is inserted. From the point of view of the logic of the situation, this may suffice, but from the dramatic need, the endless realization of known but unthought potential knowledge is hardly enough. The Day of Judgment, the expiation of sins or the realization of greater visions, is more intelligible. Dante's vision of this cosmic drama is more vital to the religion than Thomas' logic.

Pierre Duhem, the great historian of scientific concepts, has clearly indicated the antithesis between the Greek and the Christian notions of time and the debt of our modern ideas to the latter. "Here we see with perfect clarity," he says, "the irreducible opposition of ancient philosophy to our modern doctrines, to our thermodynamics which would not allow the limited world of the ancients to pass twice through the same state, to our various theories of evolution which seek to find in everything a progress towards a certain ideal term, approached but unattainable. . . . This profound change has been entirely the work of Christianity."[8]

THE RENAISSANCE OF QUANTITY AND THE MEASUREMENT OF TIME

With new interest in instruments of scientific discovery and measurement, time once more assumes an important role as a dimension of movement for which a quantitative expression must be found. Despite Kepler's mathematical teleology,[9] Galileo ruled out any explanation in terms of final causes, and limited himself to a strictly mathematical expression, based on temporal and spatial dimensions. Time reappears as the absolute continuum of a moving present, moving from past to future in an even flow. The measured is naively taken as objective.

There are difficulties connected with temporal measurement. In order to obtain a number, one must first have a unit. A quantity, that is, is the result of an observed ratio between one element (the unit) taken as measurer and another element taken as measured. Moreover, the unit should be of the same nature or quality as the thing measured. A spatial distance, for example, is better measured by counting successive yardstick positions, than by counting the number of trees growing between two points. The measure of a continuum has the advantage that a unit of arbitrarily fixed length may be set aside for the purpose, thus giving a constant which can be reapplied whenever desired. But there are two difficulties: first, there must be an established *frame of reference*, or fixed point of departure and direction for measuring, unless we wish to run the risk of measuring back and forth, in circles, or in a hit-or-miss fashion; and second, the unit and the frame of reference must remain con-

---
8. *Le système du monde*, Vol. I, p. 261.
9. Cf. Cassirer, *Substance and Function* (Chicago: The Open Court Publishing Co., 1923), p. 136. "Kepler, although he strongly defends the claims of empirical investigation against the metaphysics of substantial forms, nevertheless reverts to the mathematical teleology of Plato in his final conception of the world."

stant if the measurement is to have any value of permanency.

Moreover, the problem of measuring time presents a paradox. Time is measured by movement and movement is measured by time. In more detail, the measurement of time presumes some constant movement as unit of measure, but any movement requires a perception of temporal flow to ascertain its constancy and this perception depends upon some movement. Ordinarily, we assume that the diurnal rotation of the earth is a constant movement, but the critical nature of the problem comes to light when we undertake to check possible variations in the movement which we are taking as constant.

Isaac Barrow (1630-77), the teacher of Newton, was well aware of this difficulty. "We evidently must regard Time as passing with a steady flow," he says, "therefore it must be compared with some handy steady motion, such as the motion of the stars, and especially of the Sun and the Moon; . . . But how . . . do we know that the Sun is carried by an equal motion, and that one day is equal to another . . . ? I reply that, if the sundial is found to agree with motions of any kind of time-measuring instrument, designed to be moved uniformly by successive repetitions of its own peculiar motion, . . . then it is right to say that it registers an equable motion. It seems to follow that strictly speaking the celestial bodies are not the first and original measures of Time; but rather those motions, which are observed round about us by the senses and which underlie our experiments, since we judge the regularity of the celestial motions by the help of these. On the other hand, Time may be used as a measure of motion; just as we measure space from some magnitude, and then use this space to estimate other magnitudes commensurable with the first, i. e., we compare motions with one another by the use of time as an intermediary."[10] Barrow, we notice, has no doubt that there is a

---

10. *The Geometrical Lectures*, Lecture I. Translation by J. M. Child (Chicago: The Open Court Publishing Co., 1916), pp. 36-37.

steady temporal flow. Also rather astonishingly he thinks we trust our mechanical time-measuring instruments more than we do the celestial movements. His principal contribution, however, is found in the concept of time as an intermediary between movements; for he sees clearly that we estimate time first on the basis of certain motions, and then evaluate the velocity of other motions by temporal measure, so that we really "compare some motions with others by the mediation of time," as he puts it.

In considering the development of the Newtonian idea of absolute time, it is well to note that Barrow was a Platonist, for he also considered time as the moving image of eternity and as the manifestation of a divine nature. Barrow thus has a dual conception of time; for on the one hand it is only an intermediary by which we compare velocities, but on the other it is a unique and steady flow.

Newton likewise distinguished between absolute time or pure "duration" and relative or popular time, the latter being the actual measure of movements: day, hour, month, etc. "Absolute time, in astronomy," he says,[11] "is distinguished from relative by the equation or correction of the apparent time. For the natural days are truly unequal, though they are commonly considered as equal, and used for a measure of time; astronomers correct this inequality that they may measure the celestial motions by a more accurate time. It may be, that there is no such thing as an equable motion, whereby time may be accurately measured. All motions may be accelerated and retarded, but the flowing of absolute time is not liable to any change." Thus the idea of an absolute time is clearly recognized by Newton as purely conceptual. He well realized that man is not endowed with a special time-sense capable of indicating periods of absolute time. Man devises chronometers, as accurately as possible, to supply this lack, but there is no assurance that these do not

---

11. *Principia* I, Def. VIII, Schol. Motte trans. revised by Cajori (University of Calif. Press, 1934), pp. 7-8.

accelerate or retard. Newton considered a belief in absolute time as a necessary assumption, but there were others, contemporaries of Newton, to whom the existence of an absolute time-flow seemed purely chimerical.

To consider the most notable example, Leibniz insisted that the measured dimensions of space and time are nothing apart from actual entities. Space is only an "order of coexistences" and time an "order of successions."[12] Thus, space and time for Leibniz are practically identified with the abstract concept of *order*. Newton, to be sure, had also mentioned order;[13] but with Newton the order is really secondary to the absolute continua of space and time which permit the entities to be related or ordered within them. Leibniz, on the other hand, considers the order or set of relations as primary and the absolute continua as superfluous. He replied to Dr. Clarke that it is not necessary to suppose such an absolute frame of reference just for the sake of permitting a measuring of time and space; for, he says, "order also has its quantity [i.e., is measurable] .... Relative things have their quantity as well as absolutes: for example, ratios or proportions in mathematics, have their quantity, and are measured by logarithms, and yet they are relations. Thus, although time and space consist in relations, yet they have their quantity none the less."[14] That is to say, time and space are really measures of ratios or relations, which in turn depend upon concrete entities, thus obviating the need for assuming an absolute frame of reference. Leibniz is careful not to identify space with matter or time with motion, but he insists that, though different, space is inseparable from matter or time from motion.[15] Thus it is clear that the differ-

---

12. See in particular the letters to Clarke in answer to the latter's defense of the Newtonian position.

13. Newton, *loc. cit.*, "All things are placed in time as to order of succession; and in space as to order of situation."

14. Fifth letter to Clarke, par. 54. *The Philosophical Works of Leibniz*, Mary Morris translation, Everyman's Library (London and New York: J. M. Dent and Sons, and E. P. Dutton and Co., 1934), p. 225.

15. *Ibid.*, par. 62.

ence in point of view between Leibniz and Newton is principally over the question of the need of an absolute set of reference frames in addition to and independent of concrete entities.

Leibniz gives time and space a potential rather than an actual status. Space, he says, "is *that order*, which renders bodies capable of being situated . . . ; as *time* is *that order*, with respect to their *successive* position. But if there were no creatures, space and time would be only in the ideas of God."[16] If God alone existed, time and space "would be only in the ideas of God as mere possibilities."[17] Space, according to this view, is scarcely more than the capacity of an entity to be given a position relative to some other entity. Likewise, time is only a potential succession of instants which are themselves nothing apart from enduring entities. Time and space become mental fictions.[18]

To Clarke's interesting objection that if time were only an order of successive things, the quantity of time might become greater or less while the order of successions remained the same, Leibniz replied: "I answer that this is not so; for if the time is greater there will be more similar successive states interposed, and if it is less there will be fewer, because there is no void nor condensation nor penetration (so to speak) in times any more than in places."[19] In other words, there is an absolute number of successive states, each equal in length to the other, so that length of duration is measured by the number of successive states. But Leibniz surely realized that from the point of view of human knowledge it is a matter of pure faith that all successive states are of the same length; and we cannot *know* anything except the

---

16. Fourth letter to Clarke, par. 41. G. M. Duncan trans. (2nd ed.; New Haven: Tuttle, Morehouse, and Taylor, 1908), p. 344.
17. Fifth letter to Clarke, par. 106. Duncan trans.
18. Cf. Letter 5, par. 49: "In the case of time nothing exists but instants, and an instant is not even a part of time . . . And the analogy of time and space will make us judge that one is as ideal as the other." Morris trans., pp. 223-4.
19. *Ibid.*, par. 105. Morris trans.

number of successive states. Thus, for an absolute durational flow, Leibniz has substituted, in a sense, an absolute numerical series or order of *events* ("successive states"). This is similar to the view of Aristotle with less emphasis upon the continuum and more upon the discrete series of successive states.

With regard to infinite extension and eternal duration Leibniz has some curious inferences. Time and space being dependent upon the existence of related entities, but not attributes of those entities (rather attributes of the relations between entities), it is impossible to speak of eternity except in connection with an eternal entity. Such, of course, is God, but the infinite extension of God, and the eternal duration of God, are independent of space and time, since they are not attributes of His relationship to other entities.[20] If God existed alone, as we have seen, time and space could only exist in His ideas. Leibniz further believed that God could not have selected some particular moment for the creation of the universe, since the moment depends upon the presence of the creation. That moment would be marked as the moment of creation whenever it may have occurred, and indeed it would have thus been the same moment. Yet in his essay *On the Origination of Things,* Leibniz answers the objection that his belief in a free progress would have produced perfection long ago, by saying that "although many substances have already come to great perfection, yet owing to the infinite divisibility of what is continuous, there always remain in the abyss of things parts that are asleep, and these need to be awakened and to be driven forward into something greater and better—in a word, to a better development. Hence progress does not ever come to an end though the time be infinite."[21]

The unique world-history is thus affirmed by Leibniz

---
20. See the fifth letter to Clarke, par. 106.
21. *Ibid.,* Morris trans., p. 41.

including the Christian view of a single creation and a constant improvement or progress toward an ultimate conclusion. Only, for Leibniz, perfection is always approached, asymptotically as it were, but never reached. Among events time is measurable as an ordered arrangement of those events, but apart from events time is only the potentiality of such an arrangement. The dualism is here apparent. Quite apart from the moral character or quality of events there is the possibility of temporal measurement of their relations, but also from the point of view of eternity there is an everlasting progress.

The Search for Objectivity

The dualism of temporal character is nicely reflected in the contrast between the central temporal image for Christianity and for modern science. This contrast, which we have been tracing, comes again into prominence in the nineteenth and twentieth centuries. But in the meantime the center of the philosophical stage is held so firmly by the search for certainty and objectivity, that we must turn our attention in that direction, in order to understand what happens to the concept of time. Outside the philosophical sphere, Christian concepts persisted in unwaning vigor and the new science flourished very well on its own unquestioned assumptions. The antithesis between religion and science grew acute while the philosophical mind was groping for new axioms.

Let us digress for a moment from our central task of tracing temporal dualism, so that we may observe what was happening to the metaphysical status of time. Though the skepticism of the Renaissance was directed primarily against a decadent theology, nonetheless the new science based on quantities and measurments was not immune. For a skepticism, such as that of Montaigne, with so inclusive a motto as "Que sçais-je?" (What do I know?), could not exclude any type of knowledge. It is not that Montaigne himself was entirely a skeptic, or was concerned with a skepticism of the new-born science, but rather that the spirit of his philosophy and his age was to make so profound an impression upon subsequent thinking, that it set the stage, as it were, for the whole tenor of modern philosophy. At its very inception modern philosophy was put upon the defensive epistemologically, and its major efforts, from Descartes on, have been directed principally toward the establishment of some sort of indubitable certainties.

But modern philosophy has not only been epistemologically oriented; it has also tended to emphasize the subjective as more certain than the objective, due perhaps to the initial Cartesian shove in this direction. Renaissance skepticism had brought all naive objectivisms under the microscope of epistemological doubt, whether it was the naive objectivism of medieval theology or the naive objectivism of a science based on primary qualities. And before a new objectivism could be reconstituted, the first certainties were found in the subjective world. This stress on the subjective had the consequence of producing another effort in all types of philosophy, namely, that of discovering some assured path to objectivity. And curiously, different as they are in other respects, British Empiricism shared with Continental Rationalism and Idealism this need for escaping subjectivism.

For the problem of time, this combined skepticism and subjectivism had the same far-reaching influence which it had for all matters of ultimate knowledge. Skepticism first destroyed the simple faith in the clear Christian vision of a drama that led uniquely to the seat of judgment, to heaven or hell. The great notion of time as cumulative process, as progress and history and drama, was to wait for its reassertion upon a new concern for history and especially for the history of living forms and of human cultures which comes mainly in the nineteenth century.

But in the meantime, even the notion of an objective temporal dimension was under attack. We have already observed that Leibniz was skeptical of the absolute time and space of Newton. Space and time for Leibniz are relative to compared motions. Compared motions! These are the only genuinely objective aspects which remain, and except for these, Leibnizian time has become subjective and psychological. After all, quantitatively compared motions depend upon an assurance of simultaneity between two events, but simultaneity, as it was to be so emphatically pointed out much later, is itself relative to the observer. Hobbes goes further, for he asserts that "the present only has a being in nature," that time is merely a "phantasm" or decaying image in the mind, which represents the before and after in motions. And Descartes, in his *Principles of Philosophy*, says that time, distinguished from duration, "is only a mode of thinking that duration."[22] It was left, however, for the empiricists, for Berkeley and Hume, to eliminate all traces of temporal objectivity.[23]

The Kantian effort to escape subjectivism turned first to the question of space and time. The whole Kantian method of the *a priori* apparently occurred to Kant first in this connection. In general, Kant's great innovation was that of giving to space and time the status of necessary intuitions presupposed by any act of experiencing.

We cannot undertake here a detailed exposition of the development of Kant's views with regard to space and time or an account of his long struggle to overcome difficulties inherent in his position. Suffice it to say generally that the significant contribution of Kant is the new slant on the whole problem which was produced by the introduction of his notion of *a priori forms*. In this notion we find Kant's answer to Berkeley and Hume. For Kant asserts in prin-

---
22. *Principles*, I, 557. Haldane and Ross trans. (Cambridge University Press, 1931).
23. See Hume especially, *A Treatise on Human Nature*, Bk. I, Pt. II. Time is known only through awareness of "a succession of changeable objects."

ciple that while we may never perceive directly the *objects* behind the appearances, nonetheless there are universally valid *forms* under which all perceptions are made, and these have a certain kind of objectivity. This kind of objectivity, it will be noted, is rather the internally discovered objectivity of Idealism than the externally discovered objectivity of modern Realism.

The question whether for Kant space and time are objective or subjective is not easily answerable. On the one hand time is the "form of the inner sense" which would seem to render it quite subjective, but on the other hand it is the condition of the succession of appearances and of physical motions and must have therefore a certain independent reality.[24] Yet this conflict is only one of the difficulties encountered in the Kantian position. In his earlier view space and time are given only as single intuitions, not derived by abstraction either from particulars, as are general conceptions (e. g., "man"), or from mental activity. Kant gives no intimation[25] at first that there is a mental activity which somehow generates in us the conceptions of space and time, and yet this is precisely the view which emerges in the "Analytic," and which we may take to be the more carefully considered opinion.

Space and time, for Kant, then, are not objects at all in the sense of being objects of knowledge. We simply are led to postulate their objectivity because they are prerequisite forms of experience. "Forms" here must mean not a shape or pattern abstractable from experienced objects or events, but rather a way or manner of organizing (i. e., relating) perceptions, an arranger of experience which operates in all experiencing beings. This mental activity

---

24. See especially Gunn, *The Problem of Time*, Ch. IV, "Time in the Philosophy of Kant," pp. 114ff. Also C. B. Garnett, *The Kantian Philosophy of Space* (N. Y.: Columbia University Press, 1939), especially Chapters VI-VIII.

25. Except in the *Dissertation*, section 15. See Garnett, *Kantian Philosophy of Space*, p. 208.

may not be the simple innate idea of Plato or Descartes, but it is certainly only a dynamic form of the same. That is, if we consider "idea" as including under it also mental processes or forms of synthesizing activity, we could well call these Kantian forms "innate ideas" despite Kant's affirmations to the contrary. We are led to the conclusion that whatever may be our impression of time as a pure intuition, our real knowledge of it as a conception comes from a form of mental activity. The *source* of our knowledge at least is subjective.

It is probably more than coincidence that this initial subjectivism leads Kant to a new justification of the moral, aesthetic, and teleological beliefs of mankind. These beliefs are admitted by Kant, not on a par with our knowledge of the external phenomenal world, but as the result of our *a priori* needs. They are almost hypotheses required before there can be sane behavior. Moreover, it is also more than coincidence that he concludes with the critique of the teleological judgment. For it is paramountly the kingdom of ends which gives the ultimate meaning to our evaluational concepts; since an evaluational meaning requires directed processes. It is not so great a jump from here to the philosophies of history which flourished only a decade or two after Kant. Kant did not himself develop a temporal concept based upon his last critique, but this he might well have done. Nevertheless, the Kantian method with its justification of the *a priori*, with its initial turn towards inner sources of knowledge, with its final admission of purposiveness, has paved the way for the renewed emphasis upon directional temporal processes.

CHAPTER V

HISTORY AND SCIENCE IN MODERN THOUGHT

The ideological conflict which we have been tracing became more pronounced in the last hundred and fifty years. On the one hand, we are faced with an awakened interest in history and historical processes, which was greatly accentuated by the idea of evolution. On the other hand, the problems of science have become increasingly the problems of measurement involving temporal factors, and culminating, especially in the natural sciences, in the ideas of space-time and relativity. Let us turn to a survey, perforce rather cursory, of these two striking developments.

The Renaissance, of course, did not accomplish the complete overthrow of the Christian concept. Protestantism as well as Catholicism preserved the idea of man as the human wayfarer (e. g., *Pilgrim's Progress*); and the whole of human history was still conceived in terms of predesigned epochs. Bossuet, for example, wrote a *Discours sur l'histoire universelle*, in which he not only sought to instruct his royal charge in historical events, but also in the workings of a providential plan which gives universal meaning to mundane affairs.

However, the new humanism turned thinking more upon man himself and upon human history. Even the religious picture of Pascal, wherein man stands mid-poised in a world of infinities, is somewhat humanistic. And Pascal gave early indication of his awareness of purely human progress. "For," he says, "not only does each man advance from day to day in the sciences, but all men together make a continual progress in them as the world grows older, because the same thing occurs with the succession of men as in the different ages of a particular individual; so that the whole series of men, during the course of so many centuries should be considered as a same man who exists always and learns continually."[1] Moreover, Pascal realized that human progress is not steady; for there is a *pensée* (no. 354) which commences: "La nature de l'homme n'est pas d'aller toujours, elle a ses allées et venues." And these ups and downs, he adds, also apply to human goodness and to human inventions.

A new interest in group progress and in the improvement of society was developing. For example, it was the great vision of Spinoza to utilize the seeming security of Cartesian rationalism as the foundation for a scheme of human betterment. But unfortunately there is an apparently insurmountable obstacle in a system which attempts to explain the genesis of things in terms of a logically pre-established universe. There is something incompatible between the struggles of life and history and a universe which can be understood purely deductively. Perhaps for this reason Spinoza stands at a dividing of the ways. In France there was to develop an objective interest in social and political philosophy centering around Montesquieu, Voltaire, Rousseau, and the Encyclopedists; in Germany there is a continuation of rationalism with the new subjective emphasis inspired by Kant.

The men of the French Enlightenment produced a change in historical thinking; for they realized that cultural values have not been clearly pre-established once and for all, but are rather the products of various cultures. And we have only to remember the *Esquisse des progrès de l'esprit humain* of Condorcet in order to realize how definitely evolutional this thinking was becoming. But French interest in a philosophy of history was explanatory and reformist, not metaphysical.

German interest, on the other hand, remained metaphysical, culminating in the Hegelian philosophy of history.

---

[1]. *Fragment d'un Traité du Vide*, Opuscules, Pt. I. (Brunschvicg edition; Paris: Librarie Hachette, 18th ed.), p. 80

In Hegel's work we find the supreme effort to combine the reality of the changing, evolving world of cultural values with a belief in universal, eternal, and pre-established values. Faith in the possibility of knowing eternal values is gravely jeopardized by the realization that all value judgments are relative to some culture and some age. To transcend such relativism there must be given to us some mode of comprehending the entire scheme of development, the whole sequence of the evolution of morality. Hegel discovers this knowledge within us, as a reflection of the world-spirit, according to whose logic it is unfolding. The pattern of thesis-antithesis-synthesis, which permeates the entire universe, appears in one of its manifestations in the progression of human history. Herein we find a new "plan of Providence" and a new sort of goal, namely, the complete freedom or self-identification of human behavior with the Absolute. "As the germ bears in itself the whole nature of the tree, and the taste and form of its fruits, so do the first traces of Spirit virtually contain the whole of History."[2]

We cannot consider in detail the mass of material which the nineteenth and twentieth centuries have produced concerning history and evolution. With the work of Lamarck and Darwin there was ushered in a new interest in the laws of the evolution of life which had a far-reaching influence on speculative thought. Theories of history have been scarcely less prominent following the discoveries of the documents and monuments of antiquity, and a knowledge of the struggles of the human race over a period of four or five thousand years. This, when seen against the background of man's whole growth and of the evolution of life itself as the archaeologists and palaeontologists have pieced it together, gave room for a theory which would comprehend this entire process in a single pattern of development. As evidence of

---

2. Hegel, *Philosophy of History*, Introduction. Sibree trans. (N. Y.: P. F. Collier & Son, 1900), p. 62.

the interest in this type of theory, we shall mention a few of the outstanding philosophies of history and evolution.

The complete application of the concept of evolution to all ranges of reality is, of course, that of Herbert Spencer. He pieced together in his synthetic vision an evolution which pertained not only to living forms, but to the solar system and the earth's crust, to human society and to the human mind, and to all the products of man. His faith in a movement towards ever greater "definite, coherent, heterogeneity," as his formula states it, though broken by dissolutions in the opposite direction and temporary stages of equilibrium, is that of an optimist who sees in evolution a long-range plan of progress.

An inner evolutional struggle is implied in the Schopenhauerian *Will*, which, however, has no optimistic solution. Nietzsche, on the other hand, while retaining the emphasis upon the Will, and the consequent innerness of Schopenhauer, interprets evolution in a lustier and more optimistic fashion; for the Nietzschean Will to Power, through struggle and fiction, is evolving "higher" (i. e., more powerful) types of life.

The anthropocentric positivism of Comte has no reliance upon an inner Will or a transcending Absolute; but nevertheless, Comte did imagine three stages in the history of human mental development. These are, of course, his early religious stage, his second or metaphysical stage, and finally the scientific or positive stage. In addition to this evidence of a philosophy of history, we find Comte distinguishing the concepts of social statics and social dynamics, the one concerned with the constant conditions of society, the other with its progress or evolution. Social dynamics is, quite naturally, elaborated in the light of his law of the three stages.

The scientist's desire for laws becomes an obsession, and we find it again in the thinking of Taine, who conceived of social phenomena as explainable in terms of three factors:

race, environment, and time. But Taine recognized that the limitations of our knowledge prevent us from reducing historical causes to mathematical and mechanical formulations. The mathematician, Cournot, likewise, both in his *Essai sur les fondements de nos connaissances* (1851) and his *Considérations sur la marche des idées et des événements* (1872), distinguished history as concerned with events which contain something of the fortuitous, in contrast to mathematical science. Curiously, he was led into this line of thought by his interest in statistics and chance. History, he claimed, was neither completely accidental, for it contained some elements of an essential nature, nor was it completely determined; but, rather, a combination of the two types of event.[3]

Turning back to Germany, we find a continuing interest in the philosophy of history, following Hegel. And the characteristic German emphasis upon inner realities also makes itself manifest in these new expressions of German philosophy. As a result of this subjective tendency, and its consequent danger of relativism, a concern for the nature of value and of value judgments is interwoven with the historical theories of such thinkers as Dilthey, Rickert, Troeltsch, and Scheler. There is a common realization underlying the thinking of these men, and that is that historical knowledge depends upon the activity of making value judgments.

Dilthey, for example, calls attention to the fact that since historical knowledge involves selection, and since the act of selecting involves value judgments, historical knowledge rests upon knowledge of values. Interpretation of historical events, that is, gains meaning from our inner life, which reflects a more genuine reality than the external. Consequently, in order to assure some degree of objectivity or truth to historical knowledge, there must first be some objectivity in the inner world of meanings and values.

---

3. Cf. Henri Sée, *Science et Philosophie de l'Histoire* (Second Edition; Paris: Alcan, 1933).

Rickert, like Dilthey, is concerned in showing the dependence of historical knowledge upon knowledge of values, and in assuring to the latter some objectivity. But the greatest contribution of Rickert is certainly the clarity with which he draws the distinction between historical and scientific knowledge, scientific knowledge being concerned with generalities, historical with particulars and concrete individuals. Since history deals with individuals, Rickert is much concerned with the nature of individuality. Again it is through the notion of significance or value that he seeks a solution to this question; for a greater degree of significance gives a greater degree of individuality. There is an emphasis, too, upon the teleological character of an individual; inasmuch as the value is also an end or goal which is determining the nature of the individual.

Troeltsch attempts a more modest analysis of the value problem in historical knowledge by emphasizing the fact that values are immanent rather than transcendent. He still seeks to escape relativism of value, however, by evoking a necessary value evolution in which each cultural value, though differing from its predecessors and successors, is nonetheless part of a unified process.[4]

The nature of values, as we have already observed and shall observe in more detail later, is closely connected with the historical time-sense. Briefly, this is due to the fact that if values are considered as ideals or goals, the dramatic or historical time-sense is therefore necessary to a sense of value. This relation with value carries over from the philosophies of history into the philosophies of evolution of such men as Croce, Bergson, and S. Alexander.

Similar to Bergson's view in several respects is that of Benedetto Croce, though Croce's inspiration seems to be taken more from the ideas of Hegel. However, Croce has

---

4. For an admirable treatment of the question of value relativism and its effect upon theories of historical knowledge, see Maurice Mandelbaum, *The Problem of Historical Knowledge* (N. Y.: Liveright, 1938.)

put Hegelianism into the garb of another century. Crocean Spirit is no longer the Absolute, but rather a dynamic, historical force, creating novelty at every moment of its existence. This is reflected in Croce's notion of the "eternal present" which is a sort of cumulating historical memory, and therefore never repeated. Speaking of the effort to reduce history to laws, Croce sáys: "From this point of view, one of the conceptions that has had the greatest vogue in historical books, that of *historical circles*, is revealed as an equivocal attempt to issue forth from a double one-sidedness and a falling back into it, owing to an equivocation. Because either the series of circles is conceived as composed of identicals and we have only permanency, or it is conceived as of things diverse and we have only change. But if, on the contrary, we conceive it as circularity that is perpetually identical and at the same time perpetually diverse, in this sense it coincides with the conception of development itself."[5] History, then, is knowledge of an everchanging, yet eternal, present, which is reality, and as such, historical knowledge is the equivalent of philosophy itself. Any universal philosophy or universal history which is considered as a closed system, is a mere "cosmological romance," Croce insists. There is no prescience of absolute ends; for the eternal is not a static given, but a dynamic present which creates as it unfolds. There is, at least implied, a continuous improvement of understanding, since the Spirit, which is both artist and philosopher, continues to produce and estimate events. And in each event there is a novelty which marks its own particular freedom from any predetermination.

Bergson, similarly, in his doctrine of "creative evolution," stresses the fact of a novelty which makes of change more than a mere unrolling of already existing potentialities.

---

5. Croce, *Philosophy of the Spirit*, Pt. IV, "Theory and Historiography." Ainslie translation. (Harcourt Brace, 1921), p. 84. See also *History as the Story of Liberty*, Pt. V, Ch. I. "History Does not Repeat Itself and Does not Preserve Itself Intact." (W. W. Norton and Co., 1941.)

"Radical finalism" he classes with extreme mechanism as completely static, a condition in which all is given from beforehand. Finalism and mechanism are representatives of two poles of human thought; for the intellect must proceed both by purpose and calculation. These two tendencies are complementary and essential to thought, but, for Bergson, they are inadequate as an expression of the real process of evolution, even when taken together. He insists that the road of evolution is created as it proceeds, so that we cannot truly anticipate the future. The future is not contained in the present as a represented end, but the future will explain the present more than the present can explain the future, just as, for Croce, the cumulating present contains the past.

But any explanation of evolution, it might appear, would require some finalism, some reliance upon end-forms, which are at least potentially in the actual present creatures. Bergson, believing in a freedom which, true to French philosophy, is not just self-determination, but a real uncertainty of development, nevertheless finds it necessary to define the world as "a machine for making gods"[6]—as a process approaching nearer and nearer to the godlike. If processes can be shown to be not circular, if it contains genuine novelty, we must see evidences of getting ahead, of having changed in some non-circular way; and this means that a goal must be known against which this change can be observed.

However, both Bergson and Croce make a valiant attempt to eschew all external goals and retain only those which are internal to the stream of the evolutional or historical process. Croce says, for example, "where the end has been correctly conceived as *internal*—that is to say, all one with development itself—we must conclude that it is attained at every instant."[7] And Bergson, in addition to his characteristic remark that "the gates of the future are open,"

---

6. See Bergson, *Deux sources de la morale et de la religion* (Paris: Alcan, 1932), p. 343.
7. Croce, *Philosophy of the Spirit*, Pt. IV, p. 85.

further characterizes the future as explaining and "expanding the present." Also, in a sense, the future "must be viewed as an end as much as, and more than, a result."[8] But for Bergson, progress is only noticed in retrospect.[9] There is no clear line of progression, for this would imply predictability and a determined future. And yet all changes agree in trying to open something closed. Moreover, in another penetrating passage, Bergson develops his idea of the laws of dichotomy and double frenzy. The law of dichotomy is that "which seems to provoke the realization, by their mere dissociation, of tendencies which were first only different views of a simple tendency." And the law of double frenzy is "the necessity (*exigence*) immanent in each of the two tendencies, once realized by its separation, to be followed clear to the end,—as if there were an end!"[10] That is, even though there is no real end, there is an immanent exigency to follow each diverse tendency towards an end-goal. This habit produces an unbalanced emphasis, a neglect of the abandoned tendency, which in turn seeks its "revenge," creating conflict and drama in evolutional and historical processes. There is indeed a reminiscence of Hegel in this notion, though we must, of course, recognize Bergson's sincere effort to keep the future open.

The emergent evolutionism of Samuel Alexander, with regard to the nature of the goal, represents rather a midposition between extreme determinism and extreme indeterminism. His philosophy is more external and objective, in accordance with good British tradition; for he does not emphasize with Hegel the innerness of our knowledge of the universal dialectic, nor with Bergson the innerness of the *élan vital*. As a realist, he makes of Space-Time the stuff of the universe, and of Deity a quality which is always

---

8. Bergson, *Creative Evolution*. Mitchell trans. (N. Y.: Henry Holt & Co., 1911), p. 52.
9. *Deux sources*, p. 289.
10. *Ibid.*, p. 320.

emerging, always the next in the series of emergents. His is a philosophy of analogies. There is an analogy between the Space-Time relation and the Mind-Body relation, though to be sure Time, unlike Mind, is not an emergent. Furthermore, there are definite analogies possible between each emergent and its predecessor: life is to the inorganic, as mind is to life, etc. This gives us a pattern upon which to base a certain knowledge of the next level or "deity." On the other hand, deity is for the most part still an enigma, only knowable after its attainment. Also, be it noted, the emerging quality of deity is not God, for "God is the infinite world with its nisus towards deity."[11] Deity is partly knowable and partly an enigma, or, so far as we are concerned, partly determined and partly open.

The role of time in the philosophy of Alexander is a very curious one. As already indicated, Time is to Space as Mind is to Body. Time is "the principle of growth," "the source of movement," and, in a sense, the producer of emergents. "There is a nisus in Space-Time which, as it has borne its creatures forward through matter and life to mind, will bear them forward to some higher level of existence."[12] Thus time appears as a force which is accomplishing the achievement of a goal (deity). It is interesting to contrast this notion of time with the notion mentioned by Aristotle that time is a destructive force.

In contrast to the philosophies of Dilthey, Rickert, Troeltsch, and Scheler, it is also interesting to note that Alexander insists that deity is a quality, not a value. Since values are dependent upon human evaluations, it would be illogical, if not disrespectful, to ascribe value to deity. Deity transcends human value. Nevertheless, within each level of emergence there are goods and evils, and the next higher level is the victory of the good in the lower type over

---
11. Alexander, *Space, Time and Diety* (London: Macmillan and Co., Ltd.,), Vol. II, p. 353.
12. *Ibid.*, p. 346.

its corresponding evil. Thus "deity is the distinctive quality of the higher type of perfection in this line of forms."[13] So in a sense for Alexander also, evolution is a process which is achieving higher value.

MEASURE AND RELATIVITY

A new interest in the problem of temporal measurement has arisen with the development of the Theory of Relativity, and this has occurred without any diminishing of interest in the philosophy of history and evolution or in the historical temporal perspective. Our two major perspectives thus come into sharp contrast in modern thought; for each plays an important role in certain fields of knowledge. Moreover, much of modern philosophy has been concerned with a reconciliation of this contrast.[14]

Neither the basic idea of relativity nor the idea of time as a fourth dimension is new. The relativity of time to movement and change is in a sense much older than any concept of pure time, and the dependence of movement or change upon spatial configurations naturally connects time to space. The fundamental paradox of temporal measure arises from the fact that all temporal measurements must be *spatially* observed, so that the unit of measure and the reference frame are only indirectly perceived. This characteristic of temporal measurement is clearly described by Cassirer as follows: "From the beginning, the measurement of time must forego all sensuous helps, such as seem to stand at the disposal of the measurement of space. We cannot move one stretch of time to the place of another, and compare them in direct intuition, for precisely the characteristic element of time is that two parts of it are never given at once."[15] And Poincaré has also stressed this fact. *"We have not,"* he says,

---

13. *Ibid.*, p. 413.
14. For example, Bergson, S. Alexander, and Whitehead, to name only three.
15. Ernst Cassirer, *Substance and Function and Einstein's Theory of Relativity* (Chicago: Open Court Publishing Co., 1923), p. 145.

"*a direct intuition of the equality of two intervals of time.* The persons who believe they possess this intuition are dupes of an illusion. When I say, from noon to one the same time passes as from two to three, what meaning has this affirmation? The least reflection shows that by itself it has none at all. It will only have that which I choose to give it, by a definition which will certainly possess a certain degree of arbitrariness."[16] Plato and Aristotle assumed that the diurnal rotation was a constant. Barrow realized that temporal measure is only "estimated by spatial quantities." The hypostatization of an Absolute Time by Newton was in a way an attempt to avoid the circularity of time-measure by grounding it in an assumed absolute flow, to which the measure would more or less approximate.

In brief, the most serious difficulty in the measure of time comes from the fact that experience gives us no temporal constant, so that we are forced to depend upon a motion which is assumed uniform. But this uniformity comes from the comparison of different motions with a certain space which is held to be constant. Thus, the circumference of the earth, being taken as a constant, we can ascertain the rotational velocity in miles per second; but the second, in turn, is a division of the day, and for *its* measure we assume the constancy of the earth's velocity. The measurement of time, that is, requires a *constant* of change, but this in itself is a contradiction. If we take any velocity as a constant (e. g., the velocity of light), we are dealing with distance per time unit, so that the time unit is already presupposed. It is as Aristotle said: time is not movement and movement is not time, but they are dependent upon each other when it is a question of measurement, for time is measured by movement and movement by time.[17]

Poincaré mentions, by way of illustration, the fact that

---
16. Henri Poincaré. *The Foundations of Science.* Halsted translation (New York: The Science Press, 1921), p. 224.
17. See pp. 57-58.

astronomers believe the tides have a slowing effect on the rotation of the earth. If we are to measure this retardation, we must assume that our man-made instruments are more accurate and uniform than the movement of the earth. In the case of the pendulum, we assume that *"the duration of two identical phenomena is the same;* or that the same causes take the same time to produce the same effects." But many things may act on the pendulum to vary its motion, so that it would be better, he thinks, to say instead that "causes almost identical take almost the same time to produce almost the same effects."[18] The real meaning of the slowing of the terrestrial rotation is that it is demanded by the law of conservation of energy as a result of the friction of the tides, and as an explanation of the secular acceleration of the moon, calculated according to Newton's law. Poincaré concludes that what is really at stake is the simplicity with which the law is expressed, so that the definition implicitly adopted by the astronomers is: "Time should be so defined that the equations of mechanics may be as simple as possible. In other words, there is not one way of measuring time more true than another; that which is generally adopted is only more convenient."[19]

A consideration which plays a most important part in the matter of time-measurement, and which has been central in bringing to fruition the Theory of Relativity, is that of how we know for certain when two events are simultaneous. Since, in temporal measure, one event is measured by another, the coincidence (simultaneity) of the limiting points of one event with regard to a point in the other event must be perceived, just as the coincidence of a spatial measurer with the limit of the measured object must be perceived. The realization that there can be no favored observer, no absolute fixed system, with respect to which all other movements can be measured, and that the various movements of

---

18. Poincaré, *op. cit.,* p. 225.
19. *Ibid.,* pp. 227-8.

the observers will destroy the appearance of simultaneity in cases of distant events and rapid velocities, became the cornerstone for the new notion of relativity.

Poincaré had already realized the difficulties involved in simultaneity; for physical events separated in space or from direct perception can only be said to be simultaneous if the time for both can be measured and assumed to be common. This again depends upon the nature of the signal used in announcing the event, and the velocity of this signal (as, for example, the velocity of light). Poincaré is very emphatic in pointing out that we only assume or postulate the constancy of the velocity of light in all directions, before we can measure this velocity itself.[20] Hence, we cannot be assured of simultaneity if the signal of an event at a distance depends upon the velocity of light (and similarly with any other type of signal which takes time). "It is difficult," says Poincaré, "to separate the qualitative problem of simultaneity from the quantitative problem of the measurement of time; no matter whether a chronometer is used, or whether account must be taken of a velocity of transmission, as that of light, because such a velocity could not be measured without *measuring* time. To conclude: We have not a direct intuition of simultaneity, nor of the equality of two durations. If we think we have this intuition, this is an illusion. We replace it by the aid of certain rules which we apply almost without taking count of them."[21]

We have quoted at length from Poincaré simply because he probably foresaw with greater clarity than any other man of his generation the difficulties which confront science, particularly in questions of time and space. Further, his work foreshadows not only the ideas of Einstein, but also of such interpreters of relativity as Bergson and Cassirer. Poincaré clearly points the road toward a relativity of times with respect to physical events. He definitely places simultaneity

---
20. *Ibid.*, p. 232.
21. *Ibid.*, p. 234.

on the psychological plane. And he indicates the nature of the scientific concept which seeks always the simple and convenient law.[22] In this way, these few pages of Poincaré hint at the ideas of these three men.

The Theory of Relativity has appeared to many as the direct outcome of the difficulties involved in temporal measure. The basic idea of this relativity is, of course, that for any two inertial systems having a mutual relative motion, it is impossible to say that either is at rest or has a favored position as the basis of measurement. Since time measurement, as we have already indicated, requires a constant unit of measure and an objective frame of reference, some very interesting results follow from the realization that these elements are not absolute. The frame of reference and the limit of measure are relative to the observer, that is, to his inertial system. Moreover, the unit of measure can only be applied to the temporal continuum by some accepted simultaneities. Since the perception of these simultaneities is relative to the individual observer, giving no observer or his corresponding referential system a favored position, there can be no universally accepted measure.

To be sure, there are still constants. The velocity of light is assumed constant throughout, whether or not this assumption is warranted. Also the Lorentz-Fitzgerald transformation equations give us a constant of transformation from one referential system to another, so that the amount of apparent dislocation of our measurements between two relatively moving systems can be calculated, if the relative velocity is known. But we must recognize that there is no longer any universally valid set of temporal measurements; only the particular measurements of a given observer. Furthermore, for these assertions, it makes no difference whether we are considering only the Special Theory of Relativity which was concerned merely with uni-

---

22. See Cassirer, *op. cit.*, p. 146, note 22.

form rectilinear motion, or whether we include the General Theory which considers also accelerated and rotary motions. In either case, Einstein's notion of space and time replaces all absolutistic theories, whether they are the "absolute relations" of Leibniz or the "absolute entities" of Newton. The Theory of Relativity, says Professor Werkmeister, "is simply the doctrine that the *measured* space-time order of events in the world about us depends on the point of view from which we measure. It does not affect in any way the nature and character of the 'temporality' and 'spatiality' of our immediate experience. But Einstein's theory once more emphasizes the fact that it is man's mind which provides the schemata for an interpretation of experience; and that ultimately nothing is meaningful that cannot be correlated with such schemata."[23]

One important consequence of the Theory of Relativity has been the emphasis upon the interdependence of space and time. This has quite naturally been associated with the idea of time as a fourth dimension in a space-time continuum.[24] Non-mathematical efforts to describe the "fourth dimension" are usually based on an analogy, such as the meaning of the third dimension to a supposed two-dimensional creature. In this way we may imagine an infinity of dimensions, if we like; and indeed, mathematics has no difficulty in adding perpendicular dimensions to its systems of coördinates, so long as these are expressed analytically.

But to return to the world which we are capable of perceiving and testing, it is fairly easy to see why velocities of relative moving bodies or systems are measurable in three spatial dimensions, plus one temporal, taken together as four interchangeable dimensions, rather than in a space and time which are separate. Measure is more convenient in a single

---

23. W. H. Werkmeister, *A Philosophy of Science* (N. Y.: Harper & Brothers, 1940), p. 228.
24. This idea is not new. It was suggested to d'Alembert in 1754. See Gunn, *The Problem of Time*, pp. 206ff.

continuum, than in two somewhat questionably related continua. The measurement of velocities, the key problem in modern physics, demands a continuum of uniform motion as the basis for comparison in giving the quantifiable expression of movement. But since the movement with which physics is generally interested is that which is most easily measurable, namely of objects in space, it will be much easier if our new speed-relation-continuum is only another dimension of our single continuum.

The problem of relating dimensions is also much more easily solved mathematically than the problem of relating independent continua. In fact, it is by mathematically reducing the time dimension to the equivalent of Euclidean spatial dimensions that the development of the Theory of Relativity was permitted.[25] Palágyi, the Hungarian mathematician and philosopher, while stressing the mutual dependence of time and space in all measurements of either, insists that careful distinctions should be made between such speeds as that of the earth as against that of light, between movement and motion-transference, and between movement and perception of movement.[26] These distinctions are interesting and significant of the difficulties in reducing time to a dimension of a single space-time continuum. But though we admit that for mathematical physics the four-dimensional equations are necessary, we must agree with Professor Gunn that calling time the fourth dimension "is to speak of symbolized time and not time itself. . . . The Space-Time of Minkowski and Einstein," he continues, "is but the inevitable outcome of that view of the world begun by Galileo. Time for the mathematical physicist is and must be a measurable time. The physical time-concept is radically different from the psychological concept. The metaphysical

---

25. We refer, of course, to the work of Minkowski in replacing $-c^2 dt^2$ with $+dT^2$, where $t = T\sqrt{-1}$, and $c =$ the velocity of light, taken in time units such that it becomes unity in the new equation.

26. *Die Relativitätstheorie in der modernen Physik* (Quoted by Gunn, *op. cit.*, p. 209f.)

concept, Time, however, cannot be identified with either."[27]

Cassirer has made one of the most significant contributions in the matter of the limit and perspective of quantitative knowledge. His work, Gunn remarks, "is a brilliant attempt to set forth a general *philosophical* theory based on a radically relativist epistemology, from the standpoint of which the Einstein theory is seen as the inevitable outcome of tendencies inherent in the very nature of mathematics and physics. In a sense it would not be too much to say that Cassirer's work stands in the same relation to that of Einstein as that of Kant to Newton."[28] In general, Cassirer draws attention to the fact that scientific knowledge, which is knowledge built upon measurement, finds its real constant in the laws which guide the measurements, but that the data which are accumulated can only be used if they may be worked into a system expressed by a multiplicity of relations. The physical concept commences with a logical law, such as that of the conservation of energy, and operates in assuming this law as the basis for examining the relationships of the measurement of data. He finds in the Theory of Relativity the result of the effort to resolve physical differences (including those of space and time) to the unity of purely mathematical determinations. It is the work of physics to join the knowledge of the sensible world with the unity of mathematical forms, in order to translate the manifold of sense data into the "manifold of pure functions of form and order." Physical knowledge, according to Cassirer, is fragmentary, for it is guided by the extent to which the mathematical formalism upon which it depends allows it to express its findings in a systematic way, that is, in accordance with hypotheses and theories which must be expressed rationally.

Sir James Jeans confirms this suspicion in a striking simile. Describing the simplicity of mathematical pattern, he says: "Phenomenal nature is reduced to an array of

---
27. Gunn, *op. cit.*, p. 213. See also Cassirer, *op. cit.*, p. 454f.
28. Gunn, *op. cit.*, p. 223

events in the four-dimensional continuum, and the arrangement of these events proves to be of an exceedingly simple mathematical kind. . . . It is as though we had set out to study the fundamental texture of a picture and had found this to consist of regularly spaced dots, as in a half-tone print. We are not concerned with the meaning of the picture as a whole, which may be moral or aesthetic, or anything else; this is not the province of science. We are concerned only with the fundamental texture of the picture, which might conceivably have told us something as to its physical nature, something for instance as to the substance on which the picture was printed. But science has so far been unable to discover anything about the dots except the exceeding simplicity of their arrangement."[29] This simplicity does not mean, of course, that mathematics is itself simple, but that scientific procedure, wherever possible, has reduced phenomenal complexity to simplified relational (i. e., mathematical) expression.

We must concur with Cassirer that all knowledge is partial, being limited by the perspective or point of view. All knowledge is symbolic, that is to say, it is limited by certain basic types of abstraction or "key concepts," as we have termed them. Science is based on measure, and measure is limited to a relationship, to a unit and a reference frame. It has often been remarked that Relativity is the natural result of this procedure; for it recognizes the ultimate "resolution of the natural object into pure relations of measurement," as Cassirer has phrased it.[30] Science has come to deal with relations of events and motions, of which the space-time continuum is considered as a function. Motion becomes the ultimate with which it is concerned. What it is that is in motion cannot be measured; for the measuring itself is a motion, which gives a relation of motions. Time, viewed

---

29. Jeans, *The New Background of Science* (N. Y.: The Macmillan Co., and Cambridge University Press, 1933), pp. 289-290.
30. Cassirer, *op. cit.*, p. 446.

from the perspective of the measure of events, turns out to be a function of movement, expressible as a dimension of the frame of reference of any particular event. But the time of the universe as a whole is not expressible in this way, because the universe as a whole cannot be viewed as an event relatable to another event. Hence, concerning the nature of time from the universal point of view, we are told nothing. What we are told is that in a science based upon measurements, whose unity comes through the mathematical transformation of these measurements, there are only events which need locating with respect to their particular chosen time-scales, in order that they may be brought together in conceptual unity. Time becomes incidental to the total complexity of forms and their interrelations. These, on the other hand, are changeless and eternal; for it is in terms of them that change must be expressed. Time has again assumed the role of "a moving image of eternity." Only in this case, it is no longer the Platonic principle of imperfection which is the chaos of the universe, but it is the multiplicity of changes which do not affect the geometrical patterns by which they are measured and set in order.

The parallel between the Greeks and the Moderns is striking. For the difficulties of measure, which the former found, have been just those which cause modern science to give up its belief in the absoluteness or universality of time and space. The Greeks solved this problem by postulating a number-system intrinsic in the universe. And for us, ideas of pure mathematics applied to nature have been found more satisfactory than the models of Newtonian mechanics.[31] But this does not indicate so much that rules of measure are given us ready-made by nature as that we analyze the physical world more readily with the aid of measures. We have grown adept in the manipulation of numbers and forms.

---

31. Jeans, *op. cit.*, p. 294f.

Measured time is intelligible just insofar as it conforms to the requirements of measure. There must be at least some form of plurality in order that a measurement may be performed. This necessity of the world of experience has carried over into the conceptual world, so that we conceive any measure in terms of units and multiplicities, that is, of ratios and relations. For the measurement of time, we must assume a unit which recurs exactly as before, and which is therefore a form of repetition. But further, there must be a frame of reference or system of observation which will give the measurement a reality in the world of sense. Within such a referential system, all events may be considered as relatable to a single velocity which will give them their "time." Mathematically, the times of two such systems may be computed if their relative velocities are known. But without a constant velocity which gives, hypothetically at least, a sequence of identical and measurable units, time as measure becomes insignificant as a concept of time.

The notion of time considered as dimension, then, is created by the fact that the practical application of measure is limited to the means which man has at his disposal in making measurements, and that this, when given conceptual significance, limits the use of this concept to a world which is based on constant *relations*. This is the perspective which underlies any conceptualization of the world as physical; for the very essence of such a world is an element of constancy and permanence which will not change, but may be safely taken as the reference for all calculations.

Chapter VI

BACKGROUNDS OF THE DUAL PERSPECTIVE

We have now surveyed a number of manifestations of the meaning of time in our traditional thinking. Throughout our survey we have encountered evidences of a contrast or duality in temporal conceptualization. For the most part this duality has centered around the two perspectives of progressive transition on the one hand, and of measurable continuum on the other. But associated with the notion of progressive transition there has grown an accumulation of ideas. First there was the emphasis upon the event-quality itself and upon novelty and creativity. There was moreover an association with drama and historical-evolutional processes. Finally, these led us to the idea of value and to a bond with subjective and idealistic philosophies. Associated with the idea of the measurable continuum, on the contrary, we discovered the notions of regularly repeated interval, routine recurrences of a unit in a frame of reference, and eventually the notion of a dimension of a single space-time continuum. Whereas the first perspective has involved knowledge of an evaluational kind, this second perspective has given us knowledge of a mensurational and quantitative kind. And finally, it has been associated with objective and realistic philosophies. Before we can discuss finally the nature of time, we must glance into these associations of ideas, to see if possible what is the logic of their interconnections.

In our initial chapter we mentioned several contrasting key images of the temporal complex. Let us review these briefly. *Moment* or *instant*, as "time when," was contrasted with *duration*, or "time during which." But the notion of moment seemed to presuppose the notion of duration, especially when reduced to a "knife-edge" instant. Duration then became the ground or bare continuum upon which the other notions must be cast in order to give any meaning to it. The basic durational contrast was that of *event* and *interval*, the event being more active, the interval more inert. But the character of the *event* could not be conceived unless we introduced the notions of *novelty* and *transition*, involving an awareness of change. It was by means of these images that we were able to conceive the familiar notion of a progressive, cumulative, and hence irreversible temporal character, which is involved in the idea of before and after or past-present-future. These images also gave us the historical view wherein the event looms large. The character of the *interval*, on the other hand, involved us in the notion of temporal unit, and of regular recurrence, which made possible the concept of time as measured continuum. In the extreme, the notion of time as transition led to absolute dynamic change, and the notion of recurrent interval to absolute static permanence; but these were considered as end-concepts, meaningless and inadequate when taken by themselves.

Thus, we observe how the contrast of *event* with *interval* has involved us, through the logic of necessarily associated images, in our two fundamental perspectives. But what is the basis of the further connection between the transitional historical perspective and an *evaluational* mode of cognition, in one case; and between the perspective of the recurrent interval and a *quantitative* mode of cognition, in the other? The latter is, of course, more obvious, but the former, in particular, will take some careful consideration.

The Place of Value

We cannot indulge here in the intricacies of value theory; but, nevertheless, it will be necessary to explore the implied connection between knowledge of the evaluational type and our historical perspective of time. In the first place, we have noted that historical character is also the eventful and dramatic. The reason for this appears to be the emphasis in both cases upon a sense of effort, a striving after some goal. Whether this effort achieves its aim, or whether it is disappointed in the end, is of no consequence. What is consequential is the feeling of process dominated by a struggle toward or by a creative urge. History is the record of many such tendencies, each with its particular ambition, some larger and some smaller, some long-ranged and some short-ranged. Usually these tendencies are in conflict with other tendencies; for each individual and each organic group is a center of such activity and is always to some extent selfish in its aims. Now, it is precisely of this fabric of conflicting tendencies that drama is constructed,[1] thus giving us the basis for the connection between history and drama.

How, then, is value related to this dramatic striving? If we assume, in the ordinary manner, that value means the quality of an object or event which causes the latter to be desirable, or to produce satisfaction, or to be esteemed, we see at once that a goal, as the object of a specific conscious effort, should presumably have value for those engaged in bringing it about. Further, it appears that no condition can be genuinely a "goal" unless it does have value. Thus, in every sense of effort and striving, there must also be a sense of value. Since history is so largely composed of efforts and strivings, it becomes clear why its character implies the presence of value. Routine, habitual, repetitive processes, on the other hand, carry with them a feeling of futility and lack of accomplishment which lessens or annihilates the impression of value, though value of a highly instrumental and preservative sort may still be present.

---

[1]. For my position in this regard, see "Types of Aesthetic Appeal," *New Mexico Quarterly Review*, Vol. XII (1942), pp. 281-294.

Habits, for example, are often useful instrumentally and in holding the line, as it were, against retrogression.

In processes in which we are personally or sympathetically aware of struggle, values are implied. But let us consider longer range processes, historical or evolutional, in which there is assumed to be a cumulative or progressive quality, that is, in which novelty emerges. Does this emergent novelty imply the presence of value?[2] These are cases of novelty without any apparent desiring agent. But we are inclined to view the situation anthropomorphically, and to assume that every novelty is sought after by *some* intelligence, even though at times the novel condition may seem to be to the general detriment of mankind. ("Inscrutable are the ways of the Lord," as the saying is.) Perhaps there is no harm in this anthropomorphic view, so long as it is recognized as such; for comprehension is always proportional to our ability to extend human qualities into the universe metaphorically without their seeming inappropriate. Of course, it may be argued that cases of emergent novelty appear as values according to some other criterion of good, such as that of a more complex and efficient organism. If this were the case, it would be our own desire for this other criterion, which would endow the new condition with value, rather than the fact of novelty, and in this case we could only ascribe value to those emergents which achieved our particular goals. If, however, we generalize the notion of value, so that every emergent is valuable, whether we would desire it or not, it must be that we are assuming some unknown desiring agent. If the emergent condition appears to us as desirable, we shall go further and assume that the judgment of Nature or of the Creator is in accord with our

---

2. I am indebted to a suggestion by Professor A. J. Bahm: "Insofar as values are identified with ends, and insofar as each emergent is both an end-in-itself and a means to other ends, each emergent has or is a value." It seems to me that such a definition is acceptable if we recognize the assumption of a desiring agent beyond the normal ken of human beings. See A. J. Bahm, *The New Individualism* (Mimeographed 1943; Lubbock, Texas: Texas Technological College).

own (or *vice versa*) and that there is some fundamental affinity between us. And, on such an assumption, evolutional changes have been deemed by mankind to be leading to higher values (though man might demur, if, by a new evolutional act, *homo sapiens* were surpassed).

We have now before us the basis for the connection between value and historical-evolutional processes. Historical processes imply novelty; novelty often implies conscious striving; conscious striving implies value. As a result of this connection, we tend to treat these processes evaluationally, judging them in terms of achievement. In the sphere of historical human behavior, where our sympathetic analysis of goals and ambitions enables us to delineate motives more easily, we constantly employ such evaluations in our interpretation. But in the more cosmic and evolutional processes this mode of interpretation becomes for us hazardous and daring. It forces us to make greater assumptions about the nature of the universe. And yet we cannot abandon it, for it is our best path to the understanding of such processes.[3]

Evaluating and Measuring

Since the historical perspective involves us in an evaluational type of knowledge, whereas the dimensional conceptualization of time gives us a mensurational type, we must investigate more carefully the nature of these two cognitive modes. In the first place, all knowledge depends upon contrasts and comparisons. This is as true of measurement as it is of evaluation. Each abstraction, each selected key image, is immediately contrasted with the residue or leftover element. And being man-centered, our initial and basic key images are those which start with ourselves, extending

---

[3]. Note that on the cosmic side, especially, we must distinguish between processes which are repeated cycles, such as star-histories and processes which are continuously evolutional in the sense that they are always cumulative and progessive, and never return to an initial condition.

on the one hand our values (as we have just seen), and extending on the other hand our size (for in measuring we begin with yards, arm-lengths, and foot-lengths). The original abstraction is taken as the "key image," that is, as the basis for comparison, so that there persists a strong tendency to take one image as the key to the other even in cases in which two abstractions appear almost equal. Illustrative of this tendency is the fact, noted by Bergson in connection with the Theory of Relativity, that one system is always assumed as the fundamental frame of reference to which the others are related.[4] And even in the functional relations of mathematics, it is easier to assume that one variable is "independent" or primary, while the other is "dependent," even though ultimately they may be interchangeable.

Measuring is a type of comparing and contrasting, for before there can be measurement, some key unit must be selected with which the appropriate phenomena may be compared in regard to length or some other measurable quality. Counting may be considered as a simpler kind of measurement in which the unit is not a physical measurer but the concept of a discrete individual, which is compared progressively with a group of individuals by means of numerical symbols. For measurement, each factor in the observed situation is considered only in so far as it may be used as a unit, or as the unit may be related to it, all other factors being neglected. Hence, while the result is easily verified in the common experience of more than one observer, the knowledge achieved is of a fragmentary and specially abstractive sort. But we must hasten to add that this kind of abstraction often leads to very instructive comparisons, which give clues to similarities and differences that could not be discovered otherwise. Mensurational knowledge,

---

4. Bergson, *Durée et simultanéité*, p. 33: " . . . on n'étudie pas cette réciprocité [of two systems, S and S'] sans adopter l'un des deux termes, S ou S' comme 'système de référence': or, dès qu'un système a été ainsi immobilisé, il devient provisoirement un point de repère absolu, un succédané de l'éther."

therefore, has achieved a tremendous success, so that our sciences seek continually to express their comparisons mathematically so far as possible. Nevertheless, we must warn that some qualities and functions are not adaptable to a study by measurement. Thus, while the qualities of spatial shape and configuration may be analyzed very well by mensurational relationships, and while colors may be distinguished satisfactorily by measured frequencies of light waves; nevertheless, ethical traits cannot be significantly studied in this manner, and even colors, from the point of view of artistic expression, must be compared evaluationally.

Turning to evaluational knowledge, we find that it is based upon a judgment in which the key image, taken as the basis of comparison, is a *model*. The imagination constructs this model to represent the desirable or undesirable condition. As representative of the desirable condition it is also called a goal or *ideal*. Of course, this model is not invented out of thin air, but is based either on a simple recollection or on altered and manipulated elements taken from experience.[5] Yet the important feature of the value judgment, in contrast to that of measurement, is the fact that at least one term of the comparison must be given internally in our mental imagery. Even when present conditions are judged desirable, or when value is immediately perceived,[6] if there is a conscious awareness of the reason for value, that is, if there is a genuine value judgment, there must be a contrast with an absent condition which is considered worse. Eventually, everything which is judged evaluationally is so judged in comparison with imaginary models of better and worse conditions. Thus, when a judgment of good or bad, right or wrong, beautiful or ugly, is passed on an observable situation, it is because that situation has been compared

---
5. We mentioned the process of altering or manipulating abstractions in Chapter I. See p. 11.
6. For "perceptual value," see Philip Blair Rice, "Quality and Value," *The Journal of Philosophy*, Vol. XL (1943), pp. 337-348.

with an imagined model which is considered to have more or less value.

Evaluational knowledge, then, is like temporal awareness of time; the present moment must be contrasted with past or future moments, which we know only by recollection or anticipation. Not only this, but evaluational knowledge will necessarily involve temporal awareness to the extent that we are conscious of the temporal absence of the ideal or model. Conversely, temporal awareness very often suggests evaluational knowledge, so that it is difficult for ideas of future and past not to be in terms of better and worse. This association is well expressed in Schiller's verse:

> "Es reden und träumen die Menschen viel
> Von bessern künftigen Tagen."

Thus, we find a connection not only between history and value, but also between temporal awareness and evaluational knowledge.

Subjectivism and Objectivism

It must now be apparent why the evaluational mode of conception appears subjective whereas the mensurational mode seems objective. Measured data are externally related data, easily confirmed in the experience of various observers. But beyond this, the unit of measure and the measured object or event are often able to be compared directly in a single perception of one observer, thus giving the impression of objectivity in two senses. It is interesting in this connection that the traditional "primary qualities" (e. g., Locke's solidity, extension, figure, and mobility) are precisely the *easily measured* qualities. Small wonder that they were considered more "objective"!

Evaluational knowledge, on the other hand, since it presupposes an imaginary term, must be in part subjective. Not only is one term of the comparison private to the judger, but the chance of communicating this term precisely is extremely rare. There results a general lack of agreement among people about value judgments which is in striking contrast to the much more ready agreement obtained for measurements. It is true, of course, that the lack of agreement concerning value judgments is due to more than a flaw of communication, though this factor, I believe, plays a more considerable role than we imagine. Purely *mental* images can never be conveyed by the ordinary tools of expression without distortions, and *external* models are inadequate symbols in which each observer may see quite different traits; for varieties in past experience make refined communication extremely difficult, as we all know. Complete accord in the realm of evaluational knowledge can perhaps never be obtained, but it is approached where there exists a genuine sympathy of comprehension such that two or more individuals are enabled to imagine very similar models.

The subjectivity of evaluational knowledge explains to a great extent the fact that philosophies, which have emphasized the historical time-perspective and evaluational knowledge, are on the whole *idealistic*. For idealisms, stressing as they do, the internally derived ingredient of knowledge, are naturally oriented in this way. Empirical and *realistic* philosophies, on the other hand, quite naturally emphasize relational and quantitative knowledge, and the perspective of time as measure. It is not that there is a necessary logical connection between idealism and evaluational knowledge, or between realism and mensurational knowledge; but only that a central faith in the subjective, on the one hand, and in the objective, on the other, produces a strong affinity or confidence in each case.

Bergson may not fall into the usual pattern of the idealistic philosopher, but it is certain that his denunciation of externalized or "spatialized" concepts draws him in that direction. His key images (*durée réelle*, experience which is *perçu et vécu*, the reality of the *élan vital*, etc.) betoken a confidence in the innerness of knowledge which leads eventually to mysticism. We have observed how the German philosophies of history, from Hegel onward, being more characteristically idealisms, stress the ultimate importance of evaluational knowledge.

Even psychological studies of time, which would be highly critical of philosophical idealism, are often turned in this direction by the innerness of their interests. For example, Pierre Janet, in a series of lectures given at the Collège de France in 1927-28,[7] while criticizing Bergson for regarding time as endowed with creative power, nevertheless characterizes time as "relative to human activity." Such a view naturally orients our notion of time from the point of view of the *event*, involving us in the historical-evaluational concept. According to Janet, "all notions which man possesses are derived from his activity; they are only manners of acting and the *prises de conscience* of his activity."[8] Thus our *prises de conscience*, or initial awarenesses, orient us inevitably around action, with its resulting complex of key images. Bergson had distinguished between time as a homogeneous continuum, of which the moments are aligned in space, and *real duration*, of which the moments are heterogeneous and interpenetrating, that is, between objective and subjective time.[9] But he, of course, repudiated the former. Janet's comments upon this point are interesting. He agrees that the assimilation of time to space is inadequate, but insists that that is no reason for discarding it altogether. "This mixture of time and space," he says, "is caused by the medium of acts accompanied by expectation. We have no expectation without moving (*sans bouger*), we have expectation while doing something—which we have called the *acte du guet*, the watching for an object which one is going to seize."[10] Janet thus emphasizes the presence of a certain

---

7. Published as *L'évolution de la mémoire et de la notion du temps* (Paris: A. Chahine, 1928).
8. *Ibid.*, p. 610.
9. *Essai sur les données immédiates de la conscience* (Paris, 1888). See especially pp. 182ff.
10. Janet, *op. cit.*, p. 483.

activity in the tension of expectation. From our point of view, this is enough to cloak the time-sense with a definite event-quality, with a feeling of transition and drama, so that we are oriented immediately toward the historical-evaluational perspective. Even a psychologist, like Janet, while attempting to leave time as bare as possible, has nevertheless opened the door which will allow us to proceed toward the Bergsonian view.

A more objective thinker will have more confidence both in the realities of space and in the validity of mensurational abstraction. For example, S. Alexander places time and space about on an equal footing in his system, and as for mathematical knowledge, he considers it a legitimate generalizing substitute for our failure to attain exact intuitions.[11] Whitehead not only binds spatial and temporal features inextricably together in the event, but constantly points out that our public knowledge is that of mathematical relations.[12] And Russell, with his interest in relational knowledge, also accepts the reality of a space-time order of events.[13]

Key Images of Time and Space

We come, at last, to the investigation of our most basic antitheses, exemplified for our particular problem by the contrast of *time* and *space*. It seems possible to relate this contrast to the one which we have already delineated in the case of time alone; for the mensurational view of time has given us a sort of spatialization of time. Is there a corresponding meaning of the "temporalization of space"?

The concept of space, when refined above the level of

---

11. See *Space, Time, and Deity*, especially vol. II, p. 206.
12. See, for example, *Process and Reality* (New York: The Macmillan Co., 1929), p. 498.
13. Cf. Russell, *The Analysis of Matter* (N. Y.: Harcourt Brace, 1927), p. 254: "Thus the conclusion seems to be: Psychological time may be identified with physical time, because neither is a datum, but each is derived from data by inferences of the sort we have found elsewhere, namely, inferences which allow us to know only the logical or mathematical properties of what we infer." Cf. also pp. 286, 333-342.

immediate experiences, is, like that of time, conceptualized through certain key abstractions. First of these is *distance* or *extension*, corresponding to temporal *duration*. Next, the trait of *direction* enters, whenever a frame of reference is given. And finally, we have what may be called *permanent form*. There are others in the total complex, such as *container*, *spatial interval*, etc., but we shall not delve into them here. With regard to spatial direction, as is often pointed out, there is an arbitrariness about the order of procedure which is not the case with time. That is, purely spatial directions are reversible, whereas temporal direction is irreversible. However, the spatial notion of direction, when associated with a specific movement, as it would be in our initial awareness of it, must be taken as irreversible, and therefore as involving us in a temporal trait. It is not until we abstract the moving object, and leave a bare spatial continuum, that the order of direction no longer counts. The notion of permanent form, however, is completely antithetical to the transitional image of time. Hence, an emphasis upon the perspective of time as measure through the notion of intervaled durational dimension will lead naturally to spatial analogues, as Bergson has indicated. On the other hand, an emphasis upon space as distance with a definite direction will lead us, via the awareness of movement, to the notion of a transitional event, i. e., to a temporalized space.

May we suggest that the preference for a close integration of space and time, as in the notion of a single space-time continuum, is the result of this inner connection between perspectives. We may state it as follows: The end-concept of space as permanent form is just as devoid of meaning as the end-concept of time as pure transition. Retracting a little from these end-concepts, we must include with space the key image of directionality, and with time the key image of intervaled dimension. But in these we have respectively the temporalization of space and the spatialization of time, indicating the conceptual futility in separating time and space absolutely.

Time and space are both intellectual refinements of movement. Our initial perceptual realities consist in movements, activities, changes. From these we may proceed either toward the more obviously changing or toward the more obviously unchanging. Again there is the antithesis of interval and event, which first led us to our dual conceptualization of time. But now, instead of interval, let us consider this antithesis in a more general manner, as between *object* and *event*. *Object* here stands for a static, discrete bit of experience; that is, for a relatively permanent and individually separable entity. *Event*, as before, stands for a dynamic, discrete bit of experience, that is, for a relatively changing separable entity. Now if in contrast to these key images of discreta, we include two corresponding key images of continua, we might term the relatively static continuous or inclusive image *situation*, and the relatively dynamic continuous image *process*. Thus we have two basic contrasts: (1) the static and the dynamic, and (2) the discrete and the continuous. These seem to underlie the whole logic of our reasoning, and perhaps the whole logic of our universe as well. The term object, event, situation, and process give us the basic key images of these two contrasts. These are images, moreover, which convey the greatest impression of concreteness. The major abstractions from these are: (1) *quality* which more specifically refers to static abstractable traits, taken without regard to relations; (2) *relation*, which, though still static, stresses the matter of related parts; and (3) *function*, which does double duty as either dynamic quality or dynamic relation, depending upon the way in which it is viewed.

Now, when we are concerned with the images of *object* and *situation*, or the abstractions of *quality* and *relation*, our thinking is spatially oriented. And as we have seen throughout, even within the sphere of time alone, if we take the static images we move toward the notion of time as an intervaled dimension with the associated notions of repetition, circularity, cycle, etc. But if we increase the dynamic images we tend to conceive of time as transitional, cumulative, irreversible, with the associated notions of drama and history. We may carry this dualism even further; for mensurational and quantitative knowledge must start with the images of *situation* and *relation* to which dynamic functions are reduced when they are studied in this fashion (as in graphical presentations). But evaluational knowledge will start with the images of event, process, and a function which leads to an end-condition, which, in turn, cannot be final but only a stage in a continuously cumulative process.

Key Images and Reality

Our discussion, so far, has been primarily an effort to delineate key images. But what may we say about their truth-status? To answer this question, we shall have to delve back into an epistemological groundwork, which can be done here only in a preliminary fashion.

The key image represents an insight very near to the perceptual level, that is, to our psycho-physiological contact with the world. The key image is, however, already a focalized abstraction, usually given a simple linguistic symbol. But an abstraction is only an isolated or selected fragment of perceptual experience; and, indeed, the act of isolation is performed as part of the act of perceiving itself. Moreover, the act of isolating a fragment of experience by focusing attention upon it, does not in any way lessen the reality of that experience. We must insist, therefore, that there is nothing more fictional about an abstraction than about the immediate experience. Hence, key images, as abstractions from genuine perception, are not fictions.

Nevertheless, every abstraction is at least a reduction or simplification of reality. Every key image is a restriction upon reality. And yet it is only through key images that conceptualization is possible. It follows that the real universe is in some measure always inscrutable. But on the positive side, each key image is like a special lens, which enables us to probe into the world in some particular manner, viewing and comprehending as we go; for each key image may be used to give us a perspective upon other experiences.[14] Key images are our intellectual instruments. Some are more potent than others. Some are abstracted from a small region, others from broader regions of experience. Some are restricted, others are general. But can we be sure which ones are more genuine?

We are reminded of a suggestion of Sir James Jeans to the effect that we take off "our human spectacles" when we see the world which science portrays.[15] But many generations of men have tried to do this, only to replace the old spectacles with new ones. We must not conclude, however, that our intellectual images are distorted because of this. They could not know that they were distorted unless there were a single correct view which must be recognized as such, and with which we could compare all others. In the absence of such a view, we can only accept the perspectives which our intellect presents; for these are our conceptualized realities.

But not only is each key image the creator of a special perspective, it is also subject to an analysis for the other key images which are implicated in it (i. e., abstractable from it). These implied key images in turn may be directed back upon the original in order to view it and understand it according to the perspectives which are thus created. This is precisely what we have done with "time," which may be taken itself as a key image, but which, when analyzed, was

---

14. See "Types of Aesthetic Appeal," *New Mexico Quarterly Review*, Vol. XII, No. 3, for a further treatment of the manner in which key images create perspectives.
15. Jeans, *The New Background of Science*, p. 101.

found to have a contrasting set of key images, giving us a dual perspective of time itself.

Each perspective may be refined by limiting the field to the trait exemplified by the key image, that is, by further abstractions, until at the end of such process we reach a minimal end-concept, barren of significance. Or the abstractions themselves may be modified by extension or reduction or rearrangement of parts.[16] It is through the mental activity of abstracting, and modifying abstractions and applying these abstractions to experience that man is able to create his intellectual perspectives, which are his major hypotheses. These perspectives are subject to constant testing and alteration in the hope that ultimately they will increase understanding. We might say that those images which seem to carry us furthest, which seem to explain most, to give the clearest pictures and the deepest penetrations of meaning, are the truest. Yet not only is this a matter of faith, but eventually we shall need a more accurate criterion for significance.

We must come inevitably to a *credo* sooner or later. And at this point I must confess that my own *credo* is simply that the more perspectives we have, supplementing and augmenting each other, the better will be our true understanding of the universe. To be sure, many perspectives will conflict with each other from the point of view of strict logic. As we have seen with all our problems, if we follow one key image to its logical conclusion, wherein its antithetical images are annihilated, we reach a barren end-concept in which there is little merit and less meaning. Our perspectives resist being pushed to such extremes. In the end we must sacrifice complete consistency to the reality of a universe which, for our intellects at least, is too complex to be reduced to any such consistency. And yet, we may pursue our various perspectives to a certain point without neces-

---

16. See Chapter I, p. 11.

sarily denying others. This point is reached experimentally, by trying out each perspective, by exploring it and pursuing it further even than it should be followed. But in the end we must have the strength and the wisdom to fall back to the point of maximum significance.

It is my contention, made at present as an initial postulate, that the abstracted key images which we have underlined above are those which are most significant. The changing and the unchanging, the continuous and the discrete, these are the images which seem to probe deepest. With these contrasts we can orient ourselves spatially or temporally, mensurationally or evaluationally, repetitively or historically, objectively or subjectively, "realistically" or "idealistically." Even Realism and Idealism as philosophical schemes are excellent examples of these two basic perspectives. We can look at our world through the images of objectivity and externally given data, which we simply accept, or we can look at it through the image of internally modified understandings which create for us, because of some inherent similarity between ourselves and our universe, an accurate comprehension of reality. Why not accept both sources of knowledge? No externalist denies the subjective influence without courting absurdity, and no internalist denies the objective realities without a similar danger. It is only a matter of the extent to which we stress each source. Therefore, let us regard each as experimental, to be probed to the extreme and then retracted, to some midpoint where the perspective is still significant, without becoming barren. What time and space may be in the last analysis, or for creatures greatly dissimilar to ourselves, we do not know. What they are for us will depend upon the perspectives by which we are oriented.

Ultimately, we cannot decide between the greater validity of knowledge which is given internally and knowledge which comes to us from the outside. In this, we must agree with Kant; for Kant sought to justify both ingredients, both the inner or *a priori* and the outer or *a posteriori*, as together essential to knowledge. Also, Kant himself comes very close to a pragmatic validation of his inner ingredient. Indeed, it might be argued that his "transcendental exposition" of space and time rests upon the tacit assumption that the spatial notions of Newtonian mechanics are valid not because of their axiomatic and apodictic universality, but because of their success for the science of that day. And certainly when we come to the "regulative employment of the ideas of pure reason" and to the later Critiques, the pragmatic type of validation is well established.

The validation of the inner ingredient will, however, depend upon its nature and the way in which it is manifested. Now, since the Kantian *a priori* is not only an inner ingredient, but one which is given *from beforehand*, it has a status which will distinguish it from knowledge *abstracted* either from outer or inner perceptions. Thus, time and space, being for Kant pure *a priori* intuitions, or preconditions of perception, cannot be abstractions; for pure intuitions, it is assumed, are not empirically derived.

The contrast between time as an *a priori* intuition and time as an inner abstraction is well illustrated in the criticism of the Kantian view by the French philosophers Fouillée and Guyau, whose remarks typify the psychological abstractionism of French philosophy, especially since Condillac. Kant had said that time "is not an empirical concept that has been derived from any experience. For neither coexistence nor succession would ever come within our perception, if the representation of time were not presupposed as underlying them *a priori*."[17] To this Fouilée replies: "According to us, as according to Guyau, this is just the opposite of the real order. The animal has first, to be sure, a representation, then a succession of representations, then a representation of

---

17. *Critique of Pure Reason*, Kemp-Smith trans. (London: Macmillan and Co., Ltd., 1929), p. 74.

the representations which he has had, and this in a certain imposed order; finally this succession takes the form of time in virtue of laws such as those which cause the impression of a needle thrust into the flesh to take the form of pain."[18]

The real difference here seems to lie in the distinction between abstractions and the abstractive process itself. Abstract concepts are the result of the process, not the process. But the Kantian position may be interpreted as viewing the *a priori* element as the internal *conditioner*, in which case it would be the organizing and synthesizing factor in perception or knowledge. This organizing factor is implied in the statement of Fouillée when he mentions "laws." It is present in Locke's "mental operations." And moreover, it is not empirically derived but given as an attribute of the perceiving organism. The question, then, becomes: Are time and space derived abstractions, or forms of abstracting? Now, of course, we might define time and space in such a way that we should mean by these terms the *a priori* processes which lead us to perceive temporal and spatial attributes in experienced data, or we could mean those attributes themselves, as abstracted from others in experience. Usually we mean the latter, and though the Kantian hypothesis is a brilliant attempt to avoid some of the pitfalls which an abstractionist view must encounter, I believe we should adhere to the more usual meaning. Indeed, Kant has difficulty in maintaining his position and in leaving time and space completely unconceptualized; for strictly, as "pure intuitions" they should not be capable of conceptualization.

The Kantian hypothesis has appealed to another fact, however; namely, that *a priori* forms are universal in experience or knowledge, and this is precisely the case with the spatial and temporal factors in experience. An abstractionist view finds no difficulty in this fact, however. There is no

---

18. Guyau, *La genèse de l'idée du temps* (Paris: Alcan, 1902). From the introduction by Alfred Fouillée, p. xiv.

logical necessity for setting apart certain factors simply because they are universal and ubiquitous. Abstracting is only the act of selecting features upon which to focus attention. These features may be present in only a few experiences, or they may be present in all. Thus, it might be said that from visual perception we can always abstract light, so that light must be an *a priori* form of visual perception. But logically there can be no point at which the universalizing of an abstracted trait removes it from the realm of abstractions.[19]

Finally, abstracting presumes and requires the internal ingredient in knowledge. For the mind not only selects and isolates the features of experience, but it may alter and manipulate them, and test them out, as we have said. We cannot validate, once and forevermore, either the products of these mental processes, or the processes themselves, by resort

---

[19]. For a recent valiant support of the Kantian hypothesis, see Werkmeister, *A Philosophy of Science*, especially pp. 69-76. Following are a few quotations with our comments: "Hence, far from receiving the notion of space from 'spatial' perceptions, our consciousness, by virtue of its own nature, transforms 'points of stimulation' into perceptions of spatial forms." [But abstractionism does not require that the perception be equal to or limited to "points of stimulation"; only that the perception be a psychic product of the perceptual act. Certainly we do perceive extension, distance, shape, etc.]

"We must keep in mind that the succession of ideas is not yet an idea of succession. The latter clearly involves a synthesis of elements which transcends every particular idea of which we may be aware at any one moment." [But saying that the idea of succession presupposes a temporal synthetic activity of the mind is no more obvious than saying that the synthetic activity presupposes time. This type of argument leads to circularity unless broken by an act of faith.]

"The creative act of mind is here undeniable; and it is evident that consciousness, far from deriving the notion of time from experience by a process of abstraction, produces the 'temporality' of our experience through an act of integration, i. e., synthetically." [But no one is denying the creative act of the mind. In addition, it is difficult to distinguish an abstractional derivation of the notion of time (and space) and an integrational derivation. It may be said that the act of abstraction is analytic, whereas the act of integration is synthetic. But every act of abstractional isolation is also an act of synthetic integration; for the moment a type-trait is fragmented out, as it were, it is immediately synthesized. The very act of isolation, in excluding other traits, necessarily acts as an integration of the isolated fragments. To be sure, there is a difference in the synthesis of discreta, which become group generalizations, and in the synthesis of continua, which are homogeneous throughout (as Kant points out in the case of time and space). But this difference is due to the basic difference in the key images of *discretum* and *continuum* and offers no reason for necessarily assuming a different type of synthetic act.]

to omnipresence or universality. We can simply accept them
as the most creditable and fertile part of our intellectual kit,
as the highest mark of our human endowment.

THE NATURE OF TIME

In conclusion, what may we say of the nature of time?
Starting with an analysis of the key images associated with
the temporal regions of experience, we have emerged with
two perspectives which have led us far beyond mere temporality. It was our effort to understand and to intellectualize the crude data of temporal experience which gave us this
contrast. Time is a term for a region of experience which
is abstracted (isolated) by a key image and symbolized in
language. It is further conceptualized by noting the implicated key images, which in turn produce a contrast leading to
a dual perspective.

In way of summary, what answer may we give to our
initial questions? Of these, let us consider first the relation
of time to change. The essentially temporal qualities, it
would appear, are not to be identified with change, but are
rather abstractable concomitants of change. Were it not
for change, there could be no conceptualization of time,
remotely resembling what we actually designate by this
term. Even the notion of a pure *durational* continuum
involves the notion of an ordered succession, which in turn
involves the notion of transition and novelty. But transition
is change. Hence, change is involved in the conceptualization of time as an essential part of the reality from which
our time-concept is taken. Furthermore, according to our
premises concerning abstractions, though the concept of time
may be more highly abstract than the concept of change, it is
for that reason no less real.

Our second question concerns the nature or character of
time. The major portion of the present work has outlined a
two-fold conceptualization of time. Does this mean that

time itself is dual? If we could know time as a thing-in-itself, quite independent of our modes of conceptualization, we might discover a unified time. However, since real time is for us not separable from our conceptualization of it, we can only say that time is for us in some way dual. Time is actually both dimension and event-series. It cannot be identified totally with the event-series, as Bergson tends to do, nor with pure dimensionality, as in the usual concept of our physical sciences. Its characterization is dependent upon both of these aspects.

The temporal qualities of experience are both momentary and durative, both repetitive and cumulative, both discrete and continuous. If we try to intellectualize pure time, ridding it of all inconsistency, and leaving it as "objective" as possible, we encounter difficulties. Suppose, for example, we assume that pure objective time is repetitionless, transitionless, continuous, eternal duration. But the concept of duration, we have just said, involves transition, whereas a pure continuity would be transitionless, unless we admitted recurrences. Furthermore, if we admit only recurrent periods within which transition occurs and exclude any overall transition, time will appear finite, limited to a single universal event; for there would be no way of distinguishing one period from another. When, however, time is viewed as constantly cumulative or transitional, an infinite nature seems rather to be implied. The more we try to objectivize time, to rid it of its subjective and anthropomorphic coloring, the more it simply evaporates into nothingness. We can only conclude that there is something ultimately irreconcilable about our conceptualizing efforts. It may be that our human mode of knowing is inadequate. Or it may be that the universe is not thoroughly consistent by our standards of consistency.

Our answer to the question concerning temporal reality has been indicated. At the level of immediate experience there is a multiplicity of temporal traits. At the end of our best conceptualizing efforts, there remain at least two basic concepts, neither of which can be reduced completely to the other. Since we cannot separate them, we cannot say that one concept represents the real external time, while the other is only a subjective illusion. These concepts of dimension and event-series are as real as the immediate experiences. I shall not say that they are more or less real than these experiences, or that we proceed to or from reality when we enter into the process of conceptual refinement. My thesis has been that experience and concept are equally real so long as the process of conceptualization remains faithful to the elements found in experience. This does not limit true concepts to the restricted range of perceptual experience; for elements of the latter may be justifiably extended or reduced, the justification of such manipulation being ultimately pragmatic. It simply means that if the experiences are genuine, the abstracted concepts are just as genuine.

We have sidestepped the much vexed issue of the reality of the past and future. In the first place, the concept of moment is a generalization of present moment. It is through recollection, personal or secondary, and through anticipation or prediction that we have experience with other moments than the present one. Though the recollection and anticipation are present in consciousness, these moments cannot be identified with the present moment. They are differentiated by association with different events. If we believe in the reality of those events, then, we must believe in the reality of the associated moments, and there seems to be no valid reason for denying reality to past and future events, and limiting the reality of the universe to a mere present moment.

Furthermore, let it be observed, if we conceive of these past and future moments as differentiated, it will be by reason of the associated events, which will in turn give us the notion of time as an *event-series*. On the other hand, if we abstract the notion of "present moment" (the Aristotelian "now") from its association with different events, we are led to the notion of a temporal *continuum*. But again, we can neither dispense with the moment of awareness associated with the event, nor with the event itself which serves to differentiate moments. A pure set of events has no temporal relationships, and a pure temporal continuum has no transitional or before-after character.

The two major temporal traits, which we have incorporated into our temporal scheme, involve duration. If we limit time to a mere present, this whole scheme will either evaporate or collapse into subjective fiction. But duration is required on pragmatic grounds, at least; for it is a more potent and significant concept than mere momentaneousness.

We may conclude, then, that when we try to isolate time, and conceive it according to one or the other key image alone, it becomes barren. It cannot survive without at least one complementary key image. When viewed as intervaled duration, time becomes a dimension of the space-time continuum. When viewed as process, it is the world's history, the ages of irreversible growth which the universe is experiencing. We can neither isolate it altogether from space nor from the events of history; for these are necessary to our conceptualization. Nor can we limit it to one or the other. Irreversibility in itself is not a measurable relation of events, nor a dimension of space-time. Dimensionality in itself is not transitional or cumulative. Time is more than a space-time dimension. It is more than the event-history of the universe. It is certainly more than a mere "present," whether instantaneous or specious. It is an inescapable factor of experience and understanding alike. Our metaphysics, bent upon achieving as much completeness of understanding as possible without belying experience, must take account of both temporal perspectives, and give them each their due in the ultimate world-picture.

It is unfortunate in this day and age that each specialist tends to forget the images and perspectives of other specialists. A lack of common understanding results which may well be the ruination of man's fondest hopes. The scientist needs *measure* but the historian needs *event* and value. Science is ideally just what history is not—the knowledge of law and recurrence. History, however, is a knowledge of cumulative events. But the scientist needs to study non-repetitive processes, and the historian must not overlook the possibility of cycles.

Even within science, there is a diversity of view which is based on our two perspectives. Perhaps it is not too far-fetched to suggest that such alternative concepts of the physical world as that of matter in motion, on the one hand, and as that of centers of energy, on the other, are a reflection of this same antithesis. Biological sciences and certainly social sciences are illuminated principally by the key images of event, process, energy, and value.

As we have seen again and again, our philosophies likewise are dominated by one or the other perspective. Moreover, each philosopher, since the Greeks, has struggled with this alternative in one guise or another. But we need both philosophies. We must see the world as measured and repetitive, as body and space-time. But we must also see it as fraught with values, as history, emergent and energetic, and as operating with a certain intelligence. It is only by accepting our alternative perspectives in this way that our completest understandings may be accomplished.

INDEX

Absolute, the, 84f., 88
Absolute time and relative time (Newton), 73
Abstractions, and generalizations, 10; and the *a priori*, 120-123; levels of, 9-12; negating and manipulating, 11, 109, 118; reality of, 116-118.
Abstractionism, 121f.
Acte du guet, 112
Actuality and potentiality (Aristotle), 56, 59-62
Aeternitas and *aevum*, 70
Ages of the world, Christian, 68f.; Greek and Roman, 43n., 49, 53; Hindu, 42n., 43n.
Alexander, H. B., *God and Man's Destiny*, 67n.
Alexander, S., 87, 90-92, 113; *Space, Time, and Deity*, 91n., 113n.
Anaxagoras, 47f.
Anaximander, 38, 46
Anaximenes, 42
A posteriori, 120
A priori, forms, 79-81, 120-122; intuitions, 80
Arabic literature, 47
Aristotelian, definition of *physis*, 5; definition of time, 36, 56f., 69; Deity, 61f; dilemma, 56, 62f.; hints of evolution, 61, 61n.; idea of temporal continuum, 36, 56f.; notion of time as destructive, 25; "now," 56f., 125; potentiality and actuality, 56, 59-62; unities, 19
Aristotelianism, two world-views in, 63
Aristotle, 5, 19, 23, 36, 55-64, 69, 76, 91, 93; *Ethics*, 61; *Metaphysics*, 45n., 59, 60n.; *Physics*, 5n., 25n., 55f.
Aspect system, 31-33
Athabascan languages, 31

Babylonian doctrine of the world-year, 43n.
Babylonians, 46
Bahm, A. J., *The New Individualism*, 106n
Bantu languages, 34, 36
Bashambara, 34

Barrow, Isaac, 72f., 93; *The Geometrical Lectures*, 72n.; a Platonist, 73
Bergson, H., 87-90, 92n., 95, 108, 111-114, 124; *Creative Evolution*, 90; *Deux sources de la morale et de la religion*, 89; *Durée et simultanéité*, 108n.; *Essai sur les données immédiates de la conscience*, 112n.
Berkeley, 79
Body and mind, 91
Bonet-Maury, G., "Ages of the World (Christian)," 69n.
Bossuet, *Discours sur l'histoire universelle*, 82
Brahmanist concept of cycles, 41f.
Buddhist, concept of cycles, 42; escape, 44.

Calendars, 24-30; and the quantified concept of time, 29f.; as producing the notion of cycles, 44; astronomical, 25; ceremonial, 27; need for dates of reference in, 28; seasonal, 26
Cartesian, rationalism, 83; subjectivism, 78
Cassirer, Ernst, 33n., 34f., 38, 71n., 92, 95, 99f.; *Philosophie der Symbolischen Formen*, 33n.; *Substance and Function*, 71n., 92n.
Catholicism, 82
Chaldeans, 46
Change, and permanence, 12, 45, 50f., 88; and time, 19, 92, 123
Christ, 67
Christian, concept of time, 68; doctrine of ages, 68; idea of cosmic drama, 66-71, 78, 82; idea of single creation, 77
Cicero, 43n.
Clarke, 74f., 76n.
Comte, 85
Condillac, 120
Condorcet, *Esquisse des progrès de l'esprit humain*, 83
Constant of measurement, 72, 93-96, 99-102
Continuous, and discrete, 57, 115, 119, 122n., 124

129

Continuum, 5f., 8, 11-17, 20, 25f., 30, 33, 36, 56f., 71, 74, 76, 96, 98, 100, 103, 114f., 122n., 123f., 126
Cope, Leona, "Calendars of the Indians North of Mexico," 26n.
Cornford, F. M., 46f., *From Religion to Philosophy*, 46n.
Cosmic Drama in Christianity, 66-69, 78, 82
Cosmos, in Greek Naturalism, 49; intelligible, 47; moral explanation of, 48; perfection of, 59
Cosmogony, 39, 44
Cournot, 86
Cratylean *reductio ad absurdum*, 45
Creation according to Plato, 50
Critical dates, doctrine of (Hubert and Mauss), 41, 43f.
Croce, Benedetto, 87-89; *Philosophy of the Spirit*, 88n., 89n.
Culture, 22f.; and language, 30f.; hunting and fishing, 23f; pastoral and agricultural, 24f.
Cycles, and temporal repetition, 16, 20; concept of in Greek thought, 65; "historical circles" (Croce), 88; identical, 42; influence of calendar, 44; of alternation, 49
Cyclic, movement as representing time-pattern, 59; succession of seasons (Cassirer), 38

d'Alembert, 97n.
Danish, future tense in, 33
Dante, vision of cosmic drama of, 70
Darwin, 84
Deity in philosophy of Alexander, 90f.
Demiurge, the, 62
Descartes, 78f., 81; *Principles of Philosophy*, 79
Destiny, and fate in Greek Thought, 46; of God, 47
Determinism and fatalism, 47
Dies fasti and *nefasti* (Roman), 37
Dilthey, 86f., 91
Dimension, and frame of reference, 101f.; equivalent of measurable continuum, 5f., 20, 30, 35, 102, 126; time as the fourth dimension, 97f.
Directionality, 17, 114; in Greek philosophy, 45, 47-50, 52-56, 59-64, 66

Discrete and continuous, 57, 115, 119, 122n., 124
Drama, and history, 19, 78, 87, 103, 105, 116; of life, 24
Dramatic, mode in English, 32; transitional time-sense, 19, 24-26, 66f., 87, 103f., 113f., 123f., 126
Duhem, P., 65n., 70; *Le système du monde*, 65n., 71n.
Duration, 25f., 54, 73, 79, 103f., 114, 123-126; and momentaneousness, 13-18, 31, 103; concept of endless duration, 41-44, 76
Durational ground, 20
Durée réelle, 111f.
Dynamic and static, 18, 35, 55, 115f.

Early Greek philosophers, two basic concepts of, 45
Egyptian calendar, 29
Einstein, 95-99
Ekpyrosis, 42
Elan vital, 90, 111
Emergent, evolution, 90f.; value, 89, 91, 106, 106n.
Empedocles, 42; cosmology of, 49
Empiricism, 66, 78
Encyclopedists, 83
English language, tenses in, 32f.
End-concepts, 11f., 14f., 18, 104, 114, 118
Entelechal process, 64
Epistemological orientation of modern philosophy, 78
Erigena, 69
Eros motive, 51, 63
Eschatology, 39
Eternity, as endless duration, 41-44, 76f.; assumed, 124; concept of, 11f.; 17f.; hunger for, 5; paradox of, 18; time as moving image of, 18, 50, 55, 65, 101; timeless, 11, 50, 70
Euclidean space, 98
European time-view, contrasted with Hopi, 35
Evaluation as a mode of knowledge, 104, 109f.
Evolution, 20, 70, 82, 84f., 106f.; creative, 88-90; emergent, 90f.; in Aristotle, 61; of morality, 84; of time-concept, 21
Events, 8-10, 13-16, 28, 30, 33, 36, 64f., 68, 113-115; and intervals, 13, 104; as critical dates, 41;

fortuitous and determined, 86; in calendars, 27; measure of, 95, 97, 101; mythical, 39; transitional character of, 18, 114
Experience and concept, equally real, 125

Fatalism, 46; and determinism, 47
Fates, the, 52
Father Time, 25
Felin, Frances, and Torrey, H. B., "Was Aristotle an Evolutionist," 61n.
Finalism, radical, 89
Fletcher, Alice, 38; "The Omaha Tribe," 38n.
Flux and permanence, 45
Fouillée, A., 120f.
Four ages, in Greek mythology, 43n., 49
Four causes (Aristotle), 62
Frame of Reference, 62-65, 71, 74, 96, 100-102, 103, 108
French, Enlightenment, 83; language, tenses in, 34; philosophy, 89
Functions, as abstractions, 9, 115; dependent and independent variables in mathematical, 108

Galileo, 71, 98
Garnett, C. B., *The Kantian Philosophy of Space*, 80n
German, language, 33f.; philosophy of history, 86; rationalism, 83
God, according to Leibniz, 76; and substratum (Aristotle), 62f.; as Father and Son, 67; as Prime Mover, 63; completely eternal, 69; grace of, 66; in the philosophy of Alexander, 91; kingdom of, 68; Omaha concept of, 38; Platonic, 38, 51, 53f., 62; proofs of the existence of, 67
Godhead, 67
Godgiven drive (Plato), 51
Gods, Homeric, 47
Gospels, the, 66
Graff, W., *Language and Languages*, 31n.
Greek, concept of time, 66; concept of the timeless, 50, 70; determinism, 47; ' thought regarding cycles, 49, 65

Growth pattern, 59-61, 84; see evolution
Gunn, J. A., 67, 97-99; *The Problem of Time*, 80n., 97n.
Guyau, 120f.; *La genèse de l' idée du temps*, 121n.

Habits, 106
Hallowell, A. I., "Temporal Orientation," 27n.
Hebrew, concept of time, 66; literature, 47
Hegel, 83f., 86-90, 112; *Philosophy of History*, 84n.
Heraclitus, 43n., 47n.; doctrine of flux, 45
Hesiod, 43n., 49
Hindu, concept of time, 41f., 42n., 43n., 66; notion of heaven, 49
Historical, circles and novelty (Croce), 88; knowledge and value judgments, 86f.; perspectives, 113, 119
History, 20, 82-92, 126f.; and drama, 19, 66, 78, 87, 103, 105-107, 116; and value, 106f.; 110
Hobbes, 79
Hubert and Mauss, 39, 41, 43; *Mélanges d'histoire des religions*, 39n.
Hume, 79; *A Treatise on Human Nature*, 79n.

Ideal, model, 109f.; pattern, 50
Idealism, 70, 80, 111, 119
Idealists, 66
Indians, Aztec, 41n.; Guiana, 26; Hopi, 27, 35f; Maya, 37; Omaha, 37f.; calendars of, 26f., 37, 41n.; spatial divisions of, 40
Indo-European languages, 31-33, 35f.
Infinity, 11f.
Inge, Dean W. R., 68; *God and the Astronomers*, 68n.
Innate ideas, 81
Interval and event, 13, 18f., 25, 41, 57, 104, 114f., 126
Intuitions, space and time as (Kant), 80
Irreversibility, 59, 104, 114, 116; not a measurable relation, 126

Jeans, Sir James, 99, 117; *The New Background of Science*, 100n., 101n., 117n.

Jacobi, H., "Ages of the World (Indian)," 42n.
Jain concept of cycles, 42, 42n., 43n.
Janet, P., 112f.; *L'évolution de la mémoire et de la notion du temps*, 112n.
Judgment, day of, 70

Kant, 5, 79-81, 83, 99, 119-122, 122n.; *Critique of Pure Reason*, 120n.; *Dissertation*, 80n.
Kepler, 71
Key images and concepts, and end-concepts, 14, 114f.; basic, 107f.; of space, 114; of time, 7, 18, 100, 113-116; products of economy of thought, 22; reality of, 116-118, 123

La Flesche, Francis, "The Omaha Tribe," 38n.
Lamarck, 84
Language, and thought, 30; and culture, 30f.
Law of dichotomy and double frenzy, 90
Leibniz, 74-79, 97; *On the Origination of Things*, 76
Lévy-Bruhl, L., *Les fonctions mentales dans les sociétés inférieures*, 35n.
Linguistic time-sense, 30-36; three stages of (Cassirer), 34f.
Locke, mental operations, 121; primary qualities, 110
Lockyer, N., *The Dawn of Astronomy*, 29

Magnus annus, 43n.
Mandelbaum, M., *The Problem of Historical Knowledge*, 87n.
Manipulating abstractions, 11, 109, 118
Mathematics and physics, 99f.
Measurement, constant of, 99-102; nature of, 107-109; of time, 25, 55-59, 71f., 92-102
Miller, H., *History and Science*, 21n.
Mind, 48, 91
Minkowski, 98
Modal system, 32
Modern philosophy, epistemologically oriented, 77f.; subjectivism in, 78

Moira, 46f.
Montaigne, 77f.
Montesquieu, 83
Mooney, J., "Calendar History of the Kiowa," 27n.
Myth, character of for human thought, 37f; world as mirror of man in, 38, 40
Myth of Er, 49, 52-54

Negating abstractions, 11f.
Neoplatonism, 64f.
Newton, 72-75, 79, 93f., 99; absolute time, 73, 93; *Principia*, 73n.
Newtonian mechanics, 101, 120
Nisus, 91
Nietzschean *Will to Power*, 85
Non-Indo-European languages, temporal distinction in, 33
Nous, as reason (Anaxagoras), 47; in Neoplatonism, 64
Novelty, 50, 57, 61-63, 88, 103-106
Number, primarily ordinal, 29; two meanings of (Aristotle), 58; use of numerical symbols, 108

Object, 8f., 115
Odyssey, the, 29
Order, time as (Leibniz), 74

Palágyi, 98
Parmenidean, permanence, 12, 45; static universe, 17
Pascal, 82f.; *Fragment d'un traité du vide*, 83n.
Past-present-future, 17; reality of, 125
Patristic philosophies, 66
Patterns, ideal, 50; of change, 8f.; of growth, 59-61
Perfective and imperfective tenses, 33f.
Peripatetics, 64f.
Permanence and flux, 45
Perspectives, 7, 14, 92, 102f., 107, 117-119, 123, 127
Physics and mathematics, 99f.
Physis, 5
Pilgrim's Progress, 82
Plato, 18, 38, 43n., 48, 50-55, 62f., 71n., 81; and Aristotle, 63; ideal of intelligibility of, 55; Myth of Er, 49, 52-54; *Phaedo*, 48; *Republic*, 51; *Statesman*, 53f.;

theory of ideas, 50f.; *Timaeus*, 38, 50f.
Platonic, definition of *magnus annus*, 43n.; definition of time, 18, 50, 55, 65, 101; image of creation, 50; principle of imperfection, 101
Platonism, twofold significance of time in, 52.
Plotinus, 64f.
Poincaré, H., 93-96; *The Foundations of Science*, 93n.
Potentiality, for Aristotle, 60-62; for Leibniz, 77; of transition, 20
Primary qualities, 78, 110
Prime Mover, 63
Problems, of time, 6; of temporal measurement, 55-59; 71-77, 92-102
Process, 115
Progress, 70, 76f., 82f., 85; and eternal evolution (Leibniz), 76f.; and novelty, 106f.
Protestantism, 82
Providence, plan of in Hegelianism, 84
Psychological studies of time, 112
Pythagorean, contribution to idea of cycles, 49; doctrine of transmigration, 48; elements in Platonism, 51; image of cyclical rebirth, 52

Qualities, 8f., 115; primary, 78, 110

Rationalism, 66, 78, 83
Realism, 66, 80, 111, 119
Reason in early Greek philosophy, 47f.
Relations, 115f; constant, 102; internal and external, 9; part-whole, 8; quality-object, 9
Relativity, theory of, 92, 94, 96-100, 108
Renaissance, 69; humanism, 82; skepticism, 77f.
Repetition and recurrence, 16, 19f., 39-44, 45, 50, 53, 57-62, 64, 66, 72, 103, 105, 116, 119, 124, 127
Reversal of time, in the *Statesman* myth, 52-54
Rey, Abel, 28, 40n.; *La science orientale avant les Grecs*, 28n.

Rhythm, 39; see repetition
Rice, P. B., "Quality and Value," 109n.
Rickert, 86f., 91
Romance languages, future tense in, 33
Roth, W. E., 26; "An Introductory Study of the Arts, Crafts, and Customs of the Guiana Indians," 24n., 27n.
Rousseau, 83
Routine processes, 106; see repetition
Russell, B., *The Analysis of Matter*, 113n.
Rwiwe-speaking people, 34

Sacred, days, 37; numbers, 40
St. Anselm, *Cur Deus Homo*, 67
St. Augustine, 5, 68f.; *City of God*, 68; *Confessions*, 5, 69n.
St. Paul, 66
St. Thomas, 69f.
Sameness and novelty, 45
Sapir, E., *Language*, 31n.
Schiller, 110
Scholasticism, 66, 68f.
Schopenhauerian *Will*, 85
Science and temporal concepts, 20f.
Scientist and historian, 127
Sée, H., *Science et philosophie de l'histoire*, 86n.
Semitic, fatalism, 46f.; languages, 31
Seneca, 43n.
Simultaneity, 94-96, 108
Situation, 115f.
Smith, K. F., "Ages of the World (Greek and Roman)," 43n.
Socrates, 48
Socratic element in Platonism, 51
Sothic Cycle, 29
Space, according to Leibniz, 74f., 79; according to Kant, 79-81, 121f.; and time, 11; Euclidean, 98; key concepts of, 114
Space-time, 90f., 97f., 113, 115
Spatial analogues for time, 29f., 92, 111, 114; lacking in Hopi, 36
Spatialization of time, 29, 92, 111, 114
Statesman myth, 53f.
Static and dynamic, the, 115f.

Stoic, cyclic pattern, 44; notion of deluge and conflagration, 43n.; notion of *ekpyrosis*, 42
Spencer, H., 85
Spinoza, 83
Subjectivism in modern philosophy, 78
Substratum, 45, 56, 62f.

Taine, H., 85f.
Taylor, A. E., 53f.; *Plato, the Man and his Works*, 53n.
Tempo, 19f.; see rhythm and repetition
Temporal, continuum vs. events, 126 (see continuum); contrasts, 13-17, 103f.; measure, 25f., 55-59, 71f., 92-102; units, 29
Temporalization of space, 113f
Tense system, 31-34; development of in Indo-European, 35
Theory of relativity, 92, 94, 96-100, 108
Thomism, 69f
Thomistic synthesis of Greek and Christian thought, 69
Thucydides, 47n.
Time, and change, 19; as fourth dimension, 92, 97f.; as moving image of eternity, 18, 50, 55, 65, 101; as number of movement according to before and after, 36, 56f., 69; as order, 74-76; as phantasm, 79; intervaled nature of, 20; ordinary meanings of, 13; psychological studies of, 112; reversal of, 53f; 66
Time-concept, evolution of, 21
Timelessness, 11, 50, 70

Time-sense, dramatic transitional, 24; see dramatic and transition
Transition, 14-20, 24-26, 103f., 113f., 116, 123f., 126
Torrey, H. B., and Felin, Frances, "Was Aristotle an Evolutionist," 61n.
Troeltsch, 86f., 91

Uayeb days (Maya), 37
Unidirectionality of time, 17, 56; see directionality and irreversibility
Unit, 71, 100, 103, 108, 110
Universality of time and space, 120-122

Value, 104-107
Value judgments, and historical knowledge, 86f., 105; emergent, 106
Voltaire, 83
Vossler, Karl, 66f., *Medieval Culture*, 67n.

Wakonda, 37f
Werkmeister, W. H., *A Philosophy of Science*, 97, 122n.
Whitehead, A. N., 92n., 113; *Process and Reality*, 113n.
Whorf, B. L., 35f., 40n.; "The Relation of Habitual Thought and Behavior to Language," 35n.
World-Soul, Neoplatonic, 64

Xenophanes, 37

Zeno, paradoxes of, 45
Zeus, will of, 47

www.ingramcontent.com/pod-product-compliance
Lightning Source LLC
Chambersburg PA
CBHW030117170426
43198CB00009B/648